Reforming U.S. Financial Markets

Reforming U.S. Financial Markets

Reflections Before and Beyond Dodd-Frank

Randall S. Kroszner and Robert J. Shiller

The Alvin Hansen Symposium on Public Policy
Harvard University

edited and with an introduction by Benjamin M. Friedman

The MIT Press
Cambridge, Massachusetts
London, England

For information about special quantity discounts, please email special_sales@ mitpress.mit.edu

This book was set in Palatino by Graphic Composition, Inc. Printed and bound in the United States of America.

Library of Congress Cataloging-in-Publication Data

Alvin Hansen Symposium on Public Policy (5th : 2009 : Harvard University)
Reforming U.S. financial markets : reflections before and beyond Dodd-Frank / Randall S. Kroszner and Robert J. Shiller ; the Alvin Hansen Symposium on Public Policy, Harvard University ; edited and with an introduction by Benjamin M. Friedman.
    p. cm.
Papers and discussions presented at the fifth Alvin Hansen Symposium on Public Policy, held at Harvard University on April 30, 2009.
Includes bibliographical references and index.
ISBN 978-0-262-01545-5 (hbk. : alk. paper)
1. Finance—United States—Congresses. 2. Financial crises—United States—Congresses. 3. Global Financial Crisis, 2008–2009—Congresses.
4. United States—Economic policy—21st century—Congresses.
I. Kroszner, Randy. II. Shiller, Robert J. III. Friedman, Benjamin M.
IV. Title.
HG181.A575   2009
332.0973—dc22
                                                                    2010036380

10 9 8 7 6 5 4 3 2

In memorium
James S. Duesenberry

Contents

Introduction

Benjamin M. Friedman

The financial crisis that began in 2007 and the economic downturn that it triggered together constitute one of the most significant economic events since World War II. In many countries the real economic costs—costs in terms of reduced production, lost jobs, shrunken investment, and foregone incomes and profits—exceeded those of any prior post-war decline. In the United States the peak-to-trough decline in real output was 3.8 percent, slightly greater than the previous post-war record set in 1957–1958; unemployment did not reach the level that followed the 1981–1982 recession, but as of the time of writing it seems likely to remain abnormally high for much longer than it did then. To a significantly greater extent than is usual, the decline also affected countries in nearly all parts of the world.

It is in the financial sector, however, that this latest episode primarily stands out. The collapse of major financial firms, the decline in asset values and consequent destruction of paper wealth, the interruption of credit flows, the loss of confidence both in firms and in credit market instruments, the fear of default by counterparties, the intervention by governments and central banks—all were extraordinary both in scale and in scope, and often in form as well. As the U.S. experience illustrates, whether this episode produced the worst real economic downturn since World War II was, for many countries, a close call. But there is no question that for the world's financial system what happened was the greatest crisis since the 1930s. Large-scale and unusual events present occasions for introspection and learning, especially when they bring unwanted consequences. Even if no one is at fault for causing some event in the first place (an earthquake, for example), it is only natural to ask what might be done to mitigate the consequences should a similar catastrophe recur. When what went wrong was the result of human action, taken in human-built institutions, the question at issue is not merely containment but prevention. It is no surprise, therefore, that the 2007–? financial crisis has prompted a flood of proposals to reform the regulation of financial markets and financial institutions, both in the United States and elsewhere.

Within the U.S. financial markets in particular, much of the ensuing attention has focused on practices (in retrospect, clearly abuses) in the mortgage lending market that laid the groundwork for the crisis. Beginning in the late 1990s, increasingly lax underwriting standards—high loan-to-value ratios, back-loaded repayment schemes, little if any documentation—were both a cause and a consequence of the ongoing rise in house prices; less onerous lending conditions spurred demand for houses, while the rising value of the underlying collateral lessened concerns for borrowers' creditworthiness. Securitization of a large fraction of the newly issued loans further lessened the originators' concern for their integrity. In turn, investors in the created securities either misled themselves (for example, similarly counting on rising house prices to nullify the implications of borrowers' lack of creditworthiness) or were misled by rating agencies that carried out shoddy analysis and all the while faced serious conflicts of interest. Importantly for the ultimate economic impact of the crisis that ensued, many of the investors who bought these ill-supported securities were non-U.S. entities. In the meantime, three more general developments had rendered the U.S. financial system highly vulnerable to just this kind of collapse in the prices of heavily traded securities.

First, within the banking system the distinction between banking and trading had mostly disappeared—and not simply as a consequence of the formal repeal in 1999 of what then remained of the Depression-era Glass-Steagall separation between commercial banking and investment banking, which had largely eroded long before. Most of the large commercial banks, facing the need to raise their own capital in speculative securities markets, were increasingly relying on trading profits to enhance their returns, in effect turning themselves into hedge funds. (Otherwise they would have had little reason to retain, on their own balance sheets, shares of the mortgage-backed securities that they earned a fee by packaging and selling.) Meanwhile most of the large investment banks, which already had significant trading operations, were increasingly funding themselves with what amounted to short-term deposits.

Second, the pressure to boost the returns they provided to their shareowners also led many of these institutions to increase their leverage—the amount of assets they hold compared to the base of invested capital that supports them—to record levels. Leverage of twelve- or fifteen-to-one was not uncommon among the large U.S. commercial banks, and many investment banks had ratios of twenty-five- or even thirty-to-one. As a result, once these firms began to incur losses on their trading operations, they had little cushion with which to absorb them.

Third, the ongoing development of the market for financial derivatives—instruments based on the value of other financial instruments, which in many cases themselves depended on the value of still other financial instruments—moved beyond the role of enabling financial institutions and other investors to hedge risks that they already bear and instead provided vehicles for them to take on new, unrelated risks. As a result, many of the risks to which investors of all kinds became exposed bore little or no connection to fluctuations in any component of the economy's actual wealth, such as house prices or the value of companies issuing shares. The risks borne were, increasingly, merely one side or the other of zero-sum bets.

In light of these cumulating vulnerabilities, in retrospect it is not surprising that some catalyst would set off a serious crisis. The turnaround in house prices—declines at nearly 20 percent per annum on average across the country, and far more in some states and in many local residential markets—provided that catalyst. (Because what matters for any individual mortgage is the specific house collateralizing that one loan, greater dispersion of house price changes around a given average rate of decline worsens the probability of default.) Delinquencies and defaults increased rapidly, especially in the market for "sub-prime" mortgages. The value of securities backed by packages of these mortgages declined in value. Leveraged derivative claims against these securities declined even more. The investors who held these instruments took losses. Those investors that were highly levered financial institutions saw their capital erode, in many cases to the point of probable failure in the absence of government assistance. Banks stopped lending, and the market in which many companies regularly issued commercial paper effectively shut down. Unable to borrow, both businesses and families cut their spending. The economic downturn was under way.

The papers offered here by Randall Kroszner and Robert Shiller, together with the remarks of four commentators, explore what the United States should do to prevent the repeat of this kind of financial crisis with all the economic costs that it has imposed: What changes do we need in how we regulate our financial markets and financial institutions? To what extent ought we change government policies that were themselves in part responsible for what happened? What more fundamental changes in our financial arrangements—not just adjustments in how the same players perform the same tasks, but more far-reaching reorderings of what our markets do—should we consider?

In the summer of 2010, following a lengthy and often contentious national debate, the U.S. Congress enacted a broad set of financial reforms, embodied in the Dodd-Frank Wall Street Reform and Consumer Protection Act. Key elements of the new legislation included:

• creation of a new Financial Stability Oversight Council, comprising existing regulators, to be responsible for overseeing any financial institution or set of market circumstances determined to be likely to result in risk to the overall economy;

• a reallocation of banking oversight responsibility among the Federal Reserve System, the Comptroller of the Currency, and the Federal Deposit Insurance Corporation, among other changes requiring the Federal Reserve Board to supervise nonbank financial companies "that may pose risk to the financial stability of the United States in the event of their material financial distress or failure";

• authority for regulators to impose enhanced size- and risk-based capital and liquidity standards for those institutions deemed systemically important, and heightened capital requirements more generally, including authority to require bank holding companies with assets exceeding $50 billion to have convertible contingent equity as part of their capital structure;

• authority for the Financial Stability Oversight Council to require systemically important nonbank financial companies and large, "interconnected" bank holding companies to establish "resolutions plans" (popularly called "living wills")— that is, ready-at-hand plans for their orderly resolution in the event of illiquidity or insolvency;

• a ban, along lines proposed by former Federal Reserve chairman Paul Volcker, on banks' and bank holding companies' engaging in certain kinds of proprietary trading (but not their trading on behalf of customers), and on their sponsoring or investing in certain kinds of investment funds;

• a requirement that banks securitizing loans retain at least 5 percent of the credit risk of the created securities on their own balance sheets;

• authority for the relevant government agencies to undertake prompt and orderly resolution, outside the ordinary corporate bankruptcy procedures, of failing bank holding companies or other financial institutions (before this new legislation, the government had the authority to take over and resolve the failure of a bank but not a bank holding company, and not of an independent broker-dealer or insurance company);

• a requirement intended to result in most swap contracts, including credit default swaps (the form of derivative instrument that led to the demise of insurance company AIG in 2008, forcing the government to provide $182 billion of assistance), being settled through centralized clearing houses— thereby providing market-wide information and enhancing transparency;

• and creation of a new Bureau of Consumer Financial Protection empowered to establish and enforce standards applying, with some notable exceptions (for example, auto dealers providing financing for car purchases), to any person or institution selling a "consumer financial product or service."

Even a quick reading of the following papers by Kroszner and Shiller and the comments of the four discussants, however, makes clear that their value is not diminished by the passage of this new legislation. The issues they address are more fundamental, and the concrete proposals they offer go well beyond the scope of what Congress enacted. Dodd-Frank may or may not prove to be the end of the story for U.S. financial reform for the near- or even the medium-term future. But the surrounding debate, and the search for prophylactic restrictions on financial activity and constructive new ideas about how the financial system can better perform its central function in our economy, will not lose vitality or importance.

These papers and discussions were presented at the fifth Alvin Hansen Symposium on Public Policy, held at Harvard University on April 30, 2009.[1] In introducing these proceedings, I want to express my very sincere personal thanks, as well as the gratitude of the Harvard Economics Department, to Leroy Sorenson Merrifield and the late Marion Hansen Merrifield, together with numerous former students of Alvin Hansen, whose generosity made possible this series of public policy symposia that the Economics Department now sponsors at Harvard in Alvin Hansen's name. Their eager participation in this effort stands as testimony to the profound and positive effect that Professor Hansen had on so many younger economists.

I am also grateful to my colleagues James Duesenberry and Gregory Mankiw, who served with me on the committee that

chose the subject for this symposium; to Helen Gavel, who
helped arrange the symposium's logistics; to John Covell, for
his support in bringing these proceedings to publication; and
especially to Randall Kroszner and Robert Shiller, as well as
my three fellow discussants, for contributing their papers and
comments.

To my sorrow and that of my colleagues, Jim Duesenberry
died several months after this fifth Hansen Symposium. Jim,
along with our late colleague Richard Musgrave, also served
on the committee that first established the Alvin Hansen Symposium series nearly twenty years ago. Both were students,
colleagues, and ultimately friends of Alvin Hansen. All of us
in the Harvard Economics Department were deeply saddened
by Jim's death. This volume is dedicated to his memory.

* * *

In 1967, in his eightieth year, Alvin Hansen received the American Economic Association's Francis E. Walker medal. James
Tobin, in presenting this award, described him as follows:

Alvin H. Hansen, a gentle revolutionary who has lived to see his
cause triumphant and his heresies orthodox, an untiring scholar
whose example and influence have fruitfully changed the directions
of his science, a political economist who has reformed policies and
institutions in his own country and elsewhere without any power
save the force of his ideas. From his boyhood on the South Dakota
prairie, Alvin Hansen has believed that knowledge can improve the
condition of man. In the integrity of that faith he has had the courage
never to close his mind and to seek and speak the truth wherever
it might lead. But Professor Hansen is to be honored with as much
affection as respect. Generation after generation, students have left
his seminar and his study not only enlightened but also inspired—
inspired with some of his enthusiastic conviction that economics is a
science for the service of mankind.

Note

1. The first Alvin Hansen Symposium, in 1995, was on "Inflation, Unemployment, and Monetary Policy," with principal papers by Robert Solow and John Taylor. The second, in 1998, addressed the question "Should the United States Privatize Social Security?" and featured principal papers by Henry Aaron and John Shoven. The third, in 2002, focused on "Inequality in America," with James Heckman and Alan Kreuger taking opposing sides on what should be done. The fourth, in 2007, on "Offshoring of American Jobs," featured Jagdish Bhagwati and Alan Blinder. The papers and discussions from each of these prior symposia have also been published by the MIT Press.

1 Democratizing and Humanizing Finance

Robert J. Shiller

The world financial crisis that began with the subprime crisis in 2007 and continues today will be a historic occasion for regulatory reform. Serious instabilities and inconsistencies have been discovered in our financial system. We need to invent new rules of the game, so that the system will work better in the future and allow us to pursue our goals and inspirations with more satisfactory outcomes.

The U.S. government has been taking a large number of unusual steps to rescue the financial system and the economy from this the worst financial crisis since the Great Depression of the 1930s. These steps include the Term Auction Facility (TAF 2007), the Troubled Asset Relief Program (TARP 2008), the Public Private Investment Partnership (PPIP 2009), and the Term Asset-Backed Securities Lending Facility (TALF 2009). These were dramatic measures, accompanied by massive bailouts of private corporations, a doubling of the Federal Reserve balance sheet, and an unprecedented sudden expansion of banks' excess reserves and the money supply.

These steps are extraordinary by the standards of past recessions, and have little basis in economic theorizing that preceded the recent crisis. They seem to be ad hoc expedients, with just intuitive justifications, probably not all of them good.

Overall, we should probably be thankful to see such a degree of governmental response to the unusual economic situation we are in. Many of these measures are emergency measures to prevent the sinking of our economic ship, and if some of them turn out to be errors, still others may save us. We have also seen a number of generally less dramatic regulatory measures taken by Federal agencies, by state and local governments, and by self-regulatory organizations (SROs) outside of the government, to close gaps in regulation that contributed to the crisis. For example, since the subprime crisis began in 2007 the Securities and Exchange Commission (SEC) has strengthened its examination and oversight of broker-dealers, investment advisers, and mutual funds, and has stepped up investigations of abusive short selling. In 2008 the New York State Attorney General Andrew M. Cuomo reached an agreement with the three main securities rating agencies to eliminate the practice of "ratings shopping" in which issuers have been able to play agencies off against each other to get the most favorable rating. In 2009 the Financial Institutions Regulatory Authority, an SRO, announced a new financial education program for the general public.

In July 2010 Congress passed, and President Barack Obama signed, the Dodd-Frank Wall Street Reform and Consumer Protection Act sponsored by Senator Christopher Dodd and Representative Barney Frank, popularly known as "Dodd-Frank" or "FINREG," which launched a program of regulatory reform that is the most ambitious since the Great Depression.[1] But the Obama Administration proposals that were embodied in this Act, by their own admission, "do not represent the complete set of potentially desirable reforms in financial regulation."[2] The Act is in fact only a beginning of a dialogue on how to move our financial system into the twenty-first century.

We need to understand the issues so that we can be thoroughgoing in our reforms, and so that we can carry them even further than Dodd-Frank and other legislation has done to date. Dodd-Frank has many aspects, but it could be said that it consists largely of a reorganization of government agencies, for example, the elimination of the Office of Thrift Supervision, the creation of a Financial Services Oversight Council, the creation of a Federal Insurance Office, and the creation of a Bureau of Consumer Financial Protection. The Dodd-Frank Act barely mentions the speculative bubbles that are the ultimate cause of the crisis, and when it does it is only in the context of future studies it is authorizing. The Act says nothing about how their new agencies will recognize such problems in the future. The government proposals represent new beginnings, but we now have to think about how those who will run any of these agencies should formulate their policy.

Secretary of Treasury Timothy Geithner said the string of recent financial crises "have caused a great loss of confidence in the basic fabric of our financial system," and "To address this will require comprehensive reform. Not modest repairs at the margin, but new rules of the game."[3] But what *are* the principles of such new rules of the game?

After the ship has been stabilized, it will be necessary to consider and reevaluate the underpinnings of our economic system, and the theory and practice of our financial regulation. This paper is about those next steps, which are more important for the long run. Undoubtedly, the reform of our financial system will take many years to complete, and so some thought on the nature of this process is warranted now.

We need unifying principles for such actions to deal with the economic problems recently discovered. But really no overarching principle to deal with this crisis has been proposed.

Let me try to offer a couple of such principles; not the only principles that we should consider at this juncture of course, but important ones.

Important new regulations must serve the purpose of *democratizing* finance, that is, making the technology of finance work better for the *people*. This means creating an environment where technology is applied effectively to kinds of risks that are not managed well today, risks that impinge on the welfare of individuals and their businesses. Of course, people and only people matter to our economy, and everyone should know that. But regulation to date has not really focused as much as it should on making changes to enable the full power of financial theory to work for everyone.

Another principle is that new regulations must serve the purpose of *humanizing* finance, that is, making our financial institutions better respond to the way people actually *think and act* regarding financial institutions, so that they are really and effectively incentivized and to make it more natural for them to take proper actions to deal with risks. That means taking account of the actual incentives that are created by our financial institutions, something that economists are already wont to do, but also taking account of them in a deeper way that is cognizant of human psychology and of those behavior patterns that lead some people to get themselves into trouble, and that at other times lie behind speculative bubbles. That means that, analogous to human factors engineering taught in engineering departments, financial institutions have to be made to better work around the reality of human nature, taking account of how people are motivated and steering around human foibles. Indeed, some of the ad hoc measures in recent government policy were apparently taken based on an intuitive hypothesis about how psychology can be changed by government policy (restoring "confidence") and we just have to work at being more systematic about it for the future. Some of the elements of Dodd-Frank clearly advance the cause of democratizing and humanizing finance, as I shall discuss below. But in any event, there is still much more to be done to advance the two principles of democratizing and humanizing finance.

The current world financial crisis is substantially due to limits on our success so far at this point in history in realizing these two principles in our financial system. For example, most people have not been offered plans that would have hedged their real estate risks, but instead were advised to take out high, and increasingly, leveraged positions in local real estate, even if the amount invested was their entire life savings. Now, fifteen million Americans have negative net worth in their homes. They are literally wiped out, something that happens predictably from time to time among people who take leveraged undiversified positions. We should have known. But businesses that dealt with individuals regarding their real estate risks were not always incentivized properly to help them do better, and did not offer tools to enable them. That is, we did not democratize the lessons of finance so as to help all these relatively low income and unsophisticated home buyers.

The crisis occurred also because we did not humanize finance, did not take account of human nature. For example, the crisis happened substantially because of unrestrained bubbles, operating through various feedbacks including psychological contagion, that took place in stock markets and housing markets around the world. Monetary authorities did not take action against them, and institutions that were available for managing the risk of bubbles were not in place for most people. The crisis also occurred because regulators were not so organized as to resist the complacency encouraged by the bubbles regarding counterparty risk and systemic risks. Our economic incentives were not really properly aligned, encouraging people to rely on certain assumptions that were unexamined.

For another example, our regulations have not taken full account of public attitudes toward fairness. Cries of unfairness are a disturbing new aspect of our times. A properly functioning financial system has to be perceived as basically fair, otherwise political forces will be set in motion that inhibit its proper functioning and cause other problems as well. This means that we must listen to the people in judging what is fair; we must take account of their humanity. We must also not let quixotic notions of fairness interfere with good risk management and good incentivization.

There has been a revolution in academic finance, under the title "behavioral finance," over the last couple of decades. At its best, this revolution considers how the deep insights from the mathematical theory of finance can be effectively implemented in the real jungle of human emotions and behavior patterns. The insights from this research can help lead to a restructuring of our financial system in ways that are more cognizant of the realities of human nature and that bring out the full potential of financial theory.

One of the areas where cognitive science has been developing some interesting results is in the "theory of mind." This term actually refers to a faculty of the brain, which formulates an assessment of the thoughts, incentives, and pretenses of others; that is, a faculty that looks into, and forms a judgment, of others' minds. The human brain allocates specific areas to this faculty, just as it allocates areas to the recognition of faces or to the recognition of language. The theory of mind faculty is inherent to the proper functioning of human psychology, and it has to be inherent to good regulation. Only with the application of this faculty can regulators sort out the intent and purpose of financial innovation, so that it remains on the right course. Humanizing finance includes finding ways of organizing the activities of regulators so that they can exercise their best judgment about the motives and purposes of their clients without being held back excessively by bureaucratic structures. Modern financial theory provides a technology for the advancement of human welfare that is immensely powerful. At the core of financial theory are the principles of risk management: diversification and hedging. The theory shows that even if some risks to our economy are unavoidable, the human welfare costs of these risks can still be reduced. Also at the core of financial theory are theories of incentivization, so that people will have the impulse to do constructive work and their efforts will not be diminished by excessive moral hazard. But quirks of human nature, human misperceptions of risk and inconsistent attitudes toward risk, as shown by Daniel Kahneman, Amos Tversky, and a host of researchers in behavioral finance, show how hard it is to develop a system that does a semblance of adoption of these basic finance principles. An enlightened system of regulation is needed just to get to a crude approximation of the kind of risk management envisioned by the theory.

General Perspectives on Regulation

According to the *American Heritage Dictionary of the English Language*, which supplies the "ultimate Indo-European derivations" of words, the word regulation has Indo-European root "*reg-* To move in a straight line, with derivatives meaning 'to direct in a straight line, lead, rule.'"[4] The Latin *regula* meant straightedge or ruler, and, by extension, a rule.

By analogy, financial regulation is designed to keep financial systems moving in as closely as possible a straight line, that is, to stabilize them so they function well. Rules are inherent at meetings and games and kindergartens. One imposes rules on oneself for a purpose, for example, "I will exercise every morning, without fail." They are adopted as part of a psychological self-control mechanism. Companies and organizations adopt bylaws, and legislative bodies adopt rules of order, that have a form reflecting centuries of experience with the social psychology of people who are part of these bodies.

Government regulation takes place on a variety of levels, not only at the federal level, but also on the state and local levels. There is a coordination problem across all these different regulators, a problem that has been resolved increasingly over the history of this nation by centralizing regulation at the federal level, but state and local financial regulation still persist.

In finance, as in other areas of human activity, there are industry groups (sometimes designated SROs) which represent private interests of an industry group and set rules for their proper behavior. The government delegates authority to SROs because there is a sense that rules that serve a certain purpose are better made by people who understand that purpose. SROs and other trade organizations are essential to a functioning democracy. The government can require that an industry create an SRO; that was done, for example, with the National Association of Securities Dealers (NASD) now called the Financial Industry Regulatory Authority (FINRA). The Investment Company Act of 1940, which defined regulations for the mutual fund industry, was written in collaboration with industry representatives, and the trade organization now called the Investment Company Institute (ICI) (then with the name National Committee of Investment Companies) was created in that year to assist in the administration of that act.

Thus, any discussion of regulation should not really be centered on federal government interventions, but about finding new rules for an economy, rules that may be implemented at various governmental levels and that may also be adopted by the private sector without government intervention. It seems that some of the most serious shortcomings of regulation lie in the rigidity and arbitrariness of laws and rules within which regulators must operate. Mortgage lending regulation is an important example of this problem. Federal regulation of mortgage lenders has been divided up among the Federal Reserve, the Office of the Comptroller of the Currency, the Federal Deposit Insurance Corporation (FDIC), the Office of Thrift Supervision (OTS), the National Credit Union Administration (NCUA), and various state regulatory authorities. The fragmentation of these regulators makes it difficult for them to stop bad practices, for the regulation of one sector would only put the other sectors at a competitive advantage. The regulators did issue joint "guidances," but these tended to come late and to have little force. The five federal agencies found it difficult to address the bad lending practices that infected the subprime mortgage industry, as represented by the fact that adjustable-rate mortgages were often advertised as providing lower rates (even though those rates were temporary) and that the uptake of these mortgages was dramatically higher among people with low incomes or low credit scores (Gramlich 2007). Dodd-Frank has done relatively little to deal with this problem, consolidating only one of these five regulators.

Difficulties caused by the dispersion of mortgage regulation became apparent as the mortgage boom of 2000–2006 progressed, and there was no effective regulation of the proliferation of mortgage loans that were unsuitable. The subprime loans, including adventuresome variants such as adjustable-rate mortgages (ARMs) and the variant called option ARMs, where payments could be reduced at the discretion of the borrower, while suitable and appropriate for some people, were often issued to people for whom they were unsuitable, and there was no government regulator or SRO to stop the practice.

There has not been an industry association that could inhibit bad practices in all branches of mortgage lending nor offset some of the shortcomings of federal regulators. The Mortgage Bankers Association and the National Association of Mortgage Fiduciaries, for example, do not appear to function as effective rule setters. This situation may be because the federal government has not mandated a strong SRO for mortgage lending as it has done for the securities industry. The National Mortgage Licensing System, launched in 2008 under the direction of FINRA from the initiative of Conference of State Banking Supervisors (CSBS) and the American Association of Residential Mortgage Regulators (AARMR), may be an important step forward, if it is done well. FINRA appears to be competent in doing such things, as an SRO that maintains a licensing system for registered reps and financial advisors that has worked well in the past, at least under the conceptualizations of their duties in the past.

There has also not been an SRO that would eliminate real estate appraisal fraud. Mortgage originators have in recent years sometimes flagrantly awarded business to appraisers who will rubber stamp their valuations of homes, thus supporting the real estate bubble. In March 2008, New York Attorney General Cuomo announced an agreement with Fannie Mae and Freddie Mac to buy loans only from banks that meet the standards of a new "Home Valuation Code of Conduct" (HVCC), which is designed to reduce appraisal fraud. Since Fannie and Freddie are national organizations, the effect is to impose the HVCC nationally. Under the HVCC, lenders are prohibited from using "in-house" appraisers or crony appraisers and instead must obtain appraisers from only independent appraisal management companies (AMCs). This should help reduce the rampant appraisal fraud that helped support the housing bubble, though regulation of the appraisal management firms still needs to be improved to eliminate the continuing problem of biased or careless home appraisals. The AMCs do not yet appear to be properly incentivized to go for genuine appraisals, and are often directing clients to inexpensive or careless appraisers. Indeed, they are sometimes themselves *owned* by the mortgage originators they serve. The HVCC has not done the job yet of aligning incentives for appraisers, and some alternative structure should be considered, such as giving appraisers some financial "skin in the game" of mortgage origination, so that they will have cause to worry about the actual validity of their appraisals.[5]

Another example of the inadequacy of our regulatory framework can be found in the division of risk management regulation between the SEC and the Commodity Futures Trading Commission. Another example is the division of insurance regulation across fifty state regulators. Another is the division of insurance regulation from securities regulation. Still another example is the division of systemically important failing firms between the Federal Deposit Insurance Corporation and the bankruptcy courts. All of these regulators are dealing with rules for risk management, but with divisions that represent historical accident and with the forms that risk management took at various times in history.

So, by this principle, reregulating the financial system means overhauling it much as former Treasury Secretary Henry Paulson, in a treatise with two Treasury colleagues, recommended, so that we have "objectives-based regulation"—regulation that is aimed at major economic goals that we wish it to achieve.[6]

Among the objectives-based regulators that Paulson and his co-authors recommended would be a systemic risk regulator, a prudential financial regulator and a business conduct regulator. These designations represent objectives that are central to the issues that produced the current financial crisis.

Along these lines, President Obama and the U.S. Department of Treasury (2009) proposed that an agency be created to "identify emerging systemic risks and improve interagency cooperation." Dodd-Frank took heed of the president's proposals and created a Financial Services Oversight Council, chaired by the Treasury Secretary and including heads of major U.S. government agencies as members. Moreover, Dodd-Frank further followed the president's proposal that the Federal Reserve should be given new authority to "supervise all firms that could pose a threat to financial stability, even those that do not own banks."[7] Dodd-Frank, following some of the very words of the president's proposal, empowered a Financial Services Oversight Council to identify, subject to a 2/3 vote, financial companies for which "the nature, scope, size, scale, concentration, interconnectedness, or mix of the activities . . . could pose a threat to the financial stability of the United States."[8] Such a decision by the Council would then place financial firms under the authority of the Federal Reserve. The Federal Reserve may then establish and enforce "more stringent prudential standards" for these firms, "taking into consideration their capital structure, riskiness, complexity, financial activities (including the financial activities of their subsidiaries), size, and any other risk-related factors that the Board of Governors deems appropriate."[9] This legislation allows the enforcement of capital requirements to go beyond banks to the whole shadow banking system, and enables greater care in managing these in ways that stabilize the economy.

The organization of regulation along objectives-based lines might imply that the government should have done more than just create the assembly of government agency heads that it calls the Financial Services Oversight Council. Robert Pozen (2010) would have had a more unified council, with clearer responsibility placed on one director who has no other tasks. The Dodd-Frank Act may not have gone far enough with the consolidation of regulatory agencies.

But, on the other hand, the government must proceed carefully in merging these various financial regulators, for each of these has developed a mode of dealing with the organizations under their purview. Consolidating regulators, if done carelessly, could mean that businesses whose operations are built around certain regulatory frameworks, and regulators who understand their business needs and objectives, will cease to be viable, and cease to provide risk management services that their customers have come to expect. Indeed, Dodd-Frank, with its Financial Services Oversight Council plan, leaves existing regulators (with the exception of the Office of Thrift Supervision) intact and mostly just coordinates their activities.

International coordination of such reforms is important because otherwise financial institutions will tend to migrate to the least-regulated countries. This problem creates an important role for the G20, the Financial Stability Forum, and other international agencies.[10] This point was emphasized by the President and the U.S. Treasury (2009).

Fairness and Trust

Research in behavioral economics, notably Kahneman, Knetsch, and Thaler (1986), has shown that public notions of what is fair and what is unfair represent ancient traditions that sometimes do not make sense to economists. Public notions of fairness are sometimes quixotic, but we need to work around them if we are to maintain popular support for a modern financial economy.

The 1930s Depression was an occasion when many people doubted that capitalism could retain its public support. In 1949, when people became fearful that the economy would slip again into depression after the stimulus provided by World War II abated, columnist Sylvia Porter wrote, "And this conviction I hold above all others: If ever again we do plunge into a depression of the 1929–1932 variety, capitalism and democracy as we have known them will disappear from our land."[11]

Similar things are being said this time. The global financial crisis that began with the subprime crisis in early 2007, that picked up steam to produce a worldwide recession by December 2007, and that persists today has raised new issues of market regulation. In fact, it has been widely described as a time to reevaluate the foundations of capitalism as we know it. Talk of nationalization abounds, of forcing businesses to act in ways that are unprecedented.

The free market is one of the most important inventions in human history. It is indeed an invention, and the invention takes the form of regulation and standards enforced by some form of government. Markets and government are thus inseparable, just as the functioning of markets has to change through time.

The nature of this invention and the importance of regulation, however rudimentary, for the functioning of markets was emphasized by Karl Polanyi in his classic *The Great Transformation* (1944). He argued that until a few millennia ago trade took the form primarily of reciprocal gift-giving, with no established prices or means of exchange. One made a gift with only the hope of establishing a friendly relationship with the other party that might result in a return gift later. For markets to exist, we need to be able to separate the transaction from the relationship and formalize it, and this has always required government regulation. This means that there has to be trust in rules, trust that others one hardly knows will uphold the rules.

The current financial crisis is leading to a massive groundswell of public anger against the unfairness of our economic system. There is a strong populist reaction now. People are manifestly angry, sometimes with abusive or violent language, that business people are crooked and need to be punished.[12]

The financial crisis is itself a story, told and retold in forms that may heighten the sense of unfairness of our economic system. The bestselling book about the financial crisis currently is *House of Cards* by investigative newspaper reporter William D. Cohan. It has the subtitle *A Tale of Hubris and Wretched Excess on Wall Street*. "Wretched excess" is one of the twenty basic stories that the literary analyst Ronald Tobias says all successful literature falls into.

In *Animal Spirits* (2009), George Akerlof and I argued that such human-interest stories have a critical role in shaping macroeconomic behavior, and thus the success of economies. How this story will inhibit economic transactions is a central concern for regulators.

A Historical Perspective on Regulation

The first stock markets and the first real banks were perceived as fulfilling important functions, but at the same time the need for financial regulation became obvious. These institutions became vulnerable to serious crises that seemed to damage the whole economy, sometimes creating a negative spiral. Financial regulation goes very far back, notably to the collapse of the tulip mania in 1637 that prompted the Dutch government to shut the speculative flower market down for a while. They did this in reaction to a social-psychological event then called the *windhandel*, or "wind trade," trade irrationally based on no more substance than air. In 1720, the stock market crashes in both France and the United Kingdom led to a new word for this kind of psychological event, *bulle* or "bubble," another reference to air and lack of substance, and to a new set of regulations to try to prevent a repetition of such an event.

Historically, periods of regulatory innovation have occurred in waves, followed by long periods of relative inattention and decay of the institutions. The collapse of our financial institutions in the Great Depression of the 1930s led to a broad recognition of behavioral and systemic risks to the financial system, and to a massive increase in financial regulation. But then a period of financial and economic stability over subsequent decades helped support an intellectual drift toward belief in the natural well-functioning of markets, and to dismantling of many of the controls. This complacency, coupled with the deregulation it encouraged, led to the emergence of yet new bubbles, whose collapse brought on the current financial crisis. A new attention to regulations is necessary now.

The Great Depression of the 1930s was a period when U.S. national regulation took on a new intensity at the federal level. It is not surprising that such regulation took place, for the Depression was a time when financial institutions were seen as failing on an international level, much as they are seen today. Belief in the natural goodness of market outcomes declined. State regulators were seen as having failed in their job, given the exigencies of the Depression. They were seen as too small to do the job.

It is not possible, or desirable, for each individual state government to independently work out all the details of law regarding financial institutions. There are economies of scale to such an endeavor. The National Conference of Commissioners on Uniform State Laws (NCCUSL) was created in 1892 as a nonprofit to suggest, in cooperation with state governments, standard laws that could be adopted by many states. In 1930, in response to the financial abuses of the 1920s that had been revealed after the crash of 1929, it adopted the Uniform Sales of Securities Act of 1930. However, this act never had much impact, for it was adopted by only five jurisdictions. A more successful attempt came later, with the Uniform Securities Act of 1956, which was adopted by 37 jurisdictions, and it has been amended since and continues to be an influence on state securities regulators. But the federal government has taken over the bulk of financial regulation, and so the NCCUSL has been marginalized.

The National Association of Insurance Commissioners (NAIC) was established even earlier, in 1871, to help with the analogous problem of suggesting uniform laws to states regarding insurance. It is much more important today than the NCCUSL since the federal government has not taken over insurance regulation. The difference in approach to insurance regulation, as compared with securities regulation, is a curious accident of history. There is a federal terror insurance program, and a crop insurance program, but no general federal insurance regulation. Repeated efforts to create a national insurance regulator have met with political opposition from vested interests. However, the failure of the giant insurance company American International Group (AIG) and its need for massive federal bailouts has highlighted the systemic problems posed by insurance companies and renewed interest in federal insurance regulation. A bill for federal insurance regulation, the National Insurance Consumer Protection Act (NICPA), by Representatives Melissa Bean (D-Ill.) and

Ed Royce (R-Calif.) was introduced in April 2009. It would create an option for a national insurance charter with federal regulation. It has met with both support and opposition from different elements of the insurance industry, and as of this date there has been no action on this bill. Following recommendations from the Obama Administration, Dodd-Frank has created a Federal Insurance Office to "develop expertise, negotiate international agreements, and coordinate policy in the insurance sector,"[13] but stopped short of implementing a national insurance charter. Given the difficulty of problems posed by systemic risks and their psychological underpinnings, a federal involvement in insurance regulation (and with the systemic regulator that would be introduced by the NICPA) is desirable.

The historically biggest wave of financial regulation in the U.S. began at the federal, not state level. It began in response to the stock market crash of 1929 and the following Great Depression. Those events were substantially caused by bubbles and variations in confidence and animal spirits, which created a thorny problem for regulators, a problem so deep that it was naturally handled on the federal level.

The FDIC was introduced in 1933 in response to a huge banking crisis that resulted in the shutting down of all the nation's banking systems for a month. While the FDIC was seen as a corporation that took no tax revenue from the government, it had clear governmental regulatory authority.

The Glass-Steagall Act (Banking Act of 1933) separated commercial banks, investment banks, and insurance companies. Carter Glass, Senator from Virginia, believed that commercial banks' securities operations had caused the stock market crash of 1929, that many banks failed because of their securities operations, and that commercial banks used their knowledge as lenders to do insider trading of securities. The act was created in response to an incentive failure and a recognition of the realities of the opportunities for bad behavior when incentives are not aligned properly. The SEC was created by Congress in 1934 as the first broad federal regulator of securities. It was specified that every broker must register with the SEC, every stock exchange must register, every financial advisor must register, every public security must be registered. Registration could be denied if the SEC determined that the registration was not in accordance with its rules, but the SEC also took pains to say that registration does not constitute approval of the activities that these registrations represent. In fact, an important SEC rule is that brokers must not ever tell a client that the SEC has approved a security. The SEC is merely upholding rules, largely rules of disclosure of information.[14]

The Financial Accounting Standards Board (FASB) was officially recognized by the SEC in 1973 as an SRO to set standards for accounting. Though the SEC has had the statutory right to make accounting standards, it has preferred that there be a private sector role in it. The SEC has also set the designation of Nationally Recognized Statistical Rating Organizations (NRSROs), giving the rating agencies, which began as entirely private organizations, effective regulatory authority.

These various measures, some government, some private sector, since the Great Depression have produced a financial industry that has become highly regulated in order to take account of national economic issues.

Deregulation

A reaction against the regulation that began in the Great Depression gradually took hold as the decades went by and complacency about the problems of the Depression set in. Milton

Friedman's 1962 book *Capitalism and Freedom* presented most regulation as a ruse for special interest groups to secure their own interests, and Milton Friedman's and Anna Schwartz's book *A Monetary History of the United States* argued that the government had actually caused the Depression through the Federal Reserve's mismanagement of the money supply. Milton Friedman, formerly thought of as fringe in his conservative views, saw his influence grow. He was elected president of the American Economic Association in 1966 and won the Nobel Prize in 1976.

The conservative movement grew, and with it a desire to deregulate. The movement was expressed in the election of the Conservative Party in the United Kingdom under the leadership of Margaret Thatcher and of Ronald Reagan as U.S. president in 1980.

The Depository Institutions Deregulatory and Monetary Control Act of 1980 (signed into law under the Carter Administration) ended restrictions on the interest banks may pay on deposit and effectively ended state usury laws. A delayed effect of the latter was to make it possible for mortgage lenders to launch subprime lending by charging a high enough interest rate to offset the costs of the inevitable defaults and foreclosures. After the market began responding to the ending of restrictions there had been a need for expanding the scope of regulation to protect the integrity of the lending system. Yet the expanded regulation never came, and over time during the 1990s and into the 2000s, a "shadow banking system" of nonbank mortgage originators was allowed to develop with only minimal and incoherent regulation.

The Garn–St. Germain Depository Institutions Act of 1982 (signed into law under the Reagan Administration) completed the elimination of deposit interest rate ceilings and eliminated the statutory limit on the loan-to-value ratio. Unfortunately, the deregulation of deposit rates was not met with reregulation of the risks that depository institutions were taking, leading to the Savings and Loan Crisis which culminated in the late 1980s and the recession of 1990–1991.

The Gramm-Leach-Bliley Financial Modernization Act of 1999 effectively repealed the Glass-Steagall Act and allowed commercial banks to resume investment banking and to affiliate with insurance companies.

These deregulatory measures were not taken without protest from people who feared that they would lead to financial instability. However, the protests had no effect since there were constituencies who saw short-term personal benefit from the deregulation and no political constituency to resist the deregulation. Also, these deregulatory measures were adopted at the time of an intellectual revolution in financial theory that seemed to imply, at least as carelessly applied, that financial markets work perfectly even with little regulation.

Efficient Markets Theory as a Cause of Deregulation

The idea that financial markets work perfectly, in pooling information and in price discovery, without any need for human intervention, acquired increasing status in academic finance starting in the 1960s. According to Eugene Fama's influential 1970 review of the efficient markets hypothesis, which referenced over forty studies, almost all of them from the 1960s, "the evidence in support of the efficient markets model is extensive, and (somewhat uniquely in economics) contradictory evidence is sparse." Over the 1970s and into the 1980s the view became widely influential, and part of the foundation for a conservative revolution in economics.

The popular finance textbook *Corporate Finance* by Brealey and Myers in its second, 1984 edition, near the height of the popularity of the efficient markets hypothesis, had at its end a list of great principles of finance, and number three among them was the efficient markets theory:

> Don't misunderstand the efficient-market idea. It doesn't say that there are no taxes or costs; it doesn't say that there aren't some clever people and some stupid ones. It merely implies that competition in capital markets is very tough—there are no money machines, and security prices reflect the true underlying values of assets.
>
> Statistical tests have uncovered a few apparent inefficiencies in capital markets, but most tests support the theory. We recommend that financial managers assume that capital markets are efficient unless they have a strong, specific reason to believe otherwise. This means trusting market prices and trusting investors to recognize true economic value.[15]

They were arguing against the application of any human judgment in evaluating market prices, against any efforts to discover the strength and integrity of business plans, against any efforts to discern how particular modes of doing business fit into historical events. The suggestion was to disregard any theory of history or theory of mind in making financial judgments, and approach such judgments from a rigid framework of quantifying risks from historical returns data and constructing optimal portfolios from such quantification. This was an extreme view that would not stand the test of time. The third edition of this book, which came out in 1988, kept most of the above but dropped the line recommending placing trust in market prices. Their extreme view was already mellowing. By the time of the ninth edition (2008, now including a third author Franklin Allen) the book replaced this section with a section entitled "How Important Are the Exceptions to the Efficient-Market Theory?" which discussed speculative bubbles and irrational exuberance, and concluded that

Much more research is needed before we have a full understanding of why asset prices sometimes get so out of line with what appears to be their discounted future payoffs.[16]

This is but one example, but it seems that extreme belief in efficient markets began to fade, possibly reflecting the beginnings of behavioral finance, the public reaction to the stock market crash of 1987, and changing attitudes generally.

Even today, though, opponents of regulation often present the issue as discerning who is smarter, the government bureaucrat or the market. Clearly, they say, the market wins, since it is dominated by those who are successful and highly paid to discern the details of each security, because only the winners of this game remain. Government bureaucrats, they say, tend to be poorly paid, often political appointees who are ignorant about the markets.[17]

It is popular to dismiss government regulators as mindless bureaucrats, but from my own experience with some of them (as part of securities registration procedures) I see no less intelligence or wisdom among them than among people in the financial community in general. Many of these regulators are apparently accepting of the relatively low pay for much the same reason that school teachers and nurses are. (These people are often disrespected just as regulators are, under the assumption that their low pay is a measure of their worth, too, and it has never seemed right to me.) Regulators are people who are interested in finance, but in some cases at least do not want to accept all of the demands on them that a private sector job might require, and do not want to make what they feel are ethical compromises, such as having to sell products that they do not personally fully believe in. People sort themselves into different occupations for various reasons, some of them having to do with personality. Accountants (who may be regarded as private-sector regulators themselves) have been found, using psychological inventories, to be naturally "skeptical and critical" and to have a preference to "work in a steady orderly manner."[18]

The derogatory characterization of regulators apparently has great appeal in certain quarters, but it misses the point of regulation. It is like saying we shouldn't have a referee in a sporting event because the referees are inherently less capable at playing the game than the players are. In fact, referees are of fundamental importance to sporting events, for only when there are referees can the best players show their real talents. Referees, and a good set of rules, prevent the rough play and cheap moves that would actually compromise the abilities of the best players. Spontaneous games that children put together unsupervised on empty lots have rules too, if not a referee, and the children will sometimes spontaneously invent new rules for their own games to make them play out better. They are the prototype for the SROs that play such a big role in our economy today.

Part of good regulation is seeing through the artifices and deliberate manipulations that some in the financial sector will promote. Professional regulators develop special expertise (just as sports regulators do) to detect shenanigans and assess ethical behavior, or to distinguish behavior that is in good faith from behavior which shows artifice. Just as a referee at a soccer match will recognize that certain players are deliberately hurting others, or deliberately feigning injuries, and attempt to temper his judgments to sensibly enforce a rule of law, so too must financial regulators use their judgment as to motives and artifices.

Thus, regulation that is not excessively rigid but that depends on the judgments of skilled regulators is inherently tied up with what I have called here the humanization of finance.

Regulation done properly means applying a theory of mind and a theory of finance as only skilled regulators could do.

Deregulation as One Cause of the Current Crisis

Every major historical event has multiple causes. The same is true of the irrational exuberance that preceded the crisis. Much of the cause lies in feedback mechanisms that take the form of social epidemics, epidemics that lead to speculative bubbles, which eventually burst (Shiller 2005). But, part of the cause has also been regulatory failure.

Deregulation, coupled with deposit insurance, was a clear cause of the Savings and Loan Crisis of the 1980s. It was also an important element of the cause of the current financial crisis. Regulation did not put any brakes on the bubbles in the stock market and housing market, and then exacerbated the downswing with procyclical capital requirements on banks.

The current world financial crisis had its apparent origins in the United States, since the first signs of trouble appeared (in the summer of 2007) in the U.S. subprime loan market. There were troubles in Europe too that summer, with the failures of European hedge funds that had invested in subprime mortgages, but their failures were clearly linked to those U.S. investments. As a result, the world financial crisis is frequently blamed on the United States. Since the U.S. is viewed as the principal bastion of capitalism, the crisis is also viewed, by association, as calling into question the basic principles of capitalism. But it has not yielded any distinct alternative.

Deregulation seemed to reflect a growing complacency about systemic risks, which, just like the growth of efficient markets, was another cause of regulatory failure. After decades go by without a major systemic crisis, it is easy, too easy, to imagine that we have arrived at a structure that is immune to such risks. Regulators seemed to forget that much of regulation was meant to inhibit the growth of speculative bubbles, or waves of overconfidence and complacency. The subtle effects of the efficient markets theory were to make it seem that regulators should be focused on preventing micro-mismanagement, as if there could be nothing wrong with the market as a whole.

William McChesney Martin, the Federal Reserve Chairman from 1951 to 1970, said "The job of Federal Reserve is to take away the punchbowl just when the party gets going."[19] This suggests a model of economic booms as a form of inebriation or irrationality. Indeed, he would speak out against financial excesses. But he appears to be the last Fed chairman to do so, as the efficient markets revolution was already well formed by the time he left his position at the Fed.

Regulating Bubbles and Associated Leverage

Until recently, the "efficient markets" consensus has been that monetary authorities should take no actions against speculative bubbles. Bubbles were hardly even thought to exist, and the term "bubble" was rarely, if ever, found in the index of finance textbooks. An important human element to the functioning of financial markets was ignored, and restoring consideration of this element is important for regulation.

If bubbles do not even exist, then of course they cannot be related to corporate and household leverage. The issue regarding leverage was thought to be primarily insuring the integrity of bank deposits, and hence the integrity of the money supply. Institutions that do not have deposits subject to a bank run are thus certainly of no concern for systemic effects. Hal Scott, in an introduction to a 2005 volume he edited about capital adequacy, said: "Most important, neither securities nor insurance firms pose systemic risks concerns since they have no immediately withdrawable deposits and weak, if any, public safety nets such as deposit insurance or lender-of-last resort protections of banks."[20] He asserted that the purpose of securities firm regulation is to assure that firms individually have enough capital to liquidate in events striking that firm without losses to customers. The purpose of insurance firm regulation is to have enough capital to cover the underwriting risk, the obligation to policyholders. Unfortunately, within a few years we discovered that systemic risk is actually very important for these firms. All at once, every major investment bank in the United States was unable to continue in their present form, required massive government bailouts, and the largest insurance company, AIG, required massive government bailouts expressly to avoid systemic problems to the broader economy.[21]

This view has started to change just as the efficient markets hypothesis has lost its luster. A paper by Raghuram Rajan at the 2005 Jackson Hole Symposium, taken on right at the height of the bubble in the housing and stock markets that preceded the present recession, argued that the systemic risks that were generated by risk management measures (such as credit default swaps) that were complacent about counterparty risk posed serious dangers to the system. But his remarks were mostly ignored, a symptom of the very complacency that generated the problems.

At the 2008 Jackson Hole Symposium, Kashyap, Rajan, and Stein argued for a different system, one with countercyclical capital requirements. This means that regulators would have to be tight on bank capital standards in a boom, when there is the greatest need to constrain the bubble, and then looser when the economy is in systemic stress. They further argued that banks should arrange for a contingent capital infusion (backed up by securities in a "lock box") that would become

available in the event of a systemic economic crisis, as a sort
of economic disaster insurance. Doing this is a sort of hedging
of bubble risk.

Hyun Song Shin (2008, 2009) has modeled the systemic instabilities in a leveraged banking system and feedbacks that
can cause amplified reactions to news. He has argued that the
monetary authority needs to take account of this mechanism
and lean against leverage cycles when they begin. Fostel and
Geanakoplos (2008) have modeled a leverage cycle, and argued for government interventions to reduce it.

These papers do not emphasize behavioral economics, but
some of their devices may be formal ways of representing
psychological effects, as I interpret them. Fostel and Geanakoplos model people as having different priors, with the op-
timists gaining further market presence in the upswing of a
leverage cycle. But, then, if one asks why they have different
priors, one may then be pushed back into some behavioral
economics considerations.

Michael Goldberg and Roman Frydman (2009) argue that
governments should consider imposing time-varying margin requirements separately on long purchases and on short
sales, in an effort to stabilize the market when it is undergo-
ing speculative instability. The Fed could for example lower
margin requirements on purchases and raise margin requirements on short sales at times of a bursting of a bubble. It actually pursued such a policy during the Depression, long before
the efficient markets hypothesis was dominant in academic
circles.[22] But the Fed would not do any such thing during the
recent boom, because its respect for market prices reached
pathological levels.

In an amazing suspension of long-held free market principles, the U.S. government banned short sales for a long list
of stocks in September 2008. Short sales had been considered

part of the normal operation of a financial system. As long ago as 1977, Edward Miller argued that financial markets cannot be efficient if short sales are not allowed, since without them there would be nothing to stop a small group of zealous and ill-informed investors from bidding up the prices so that they are manifestly too high to any informed people. Then, in a reversal, the government abandoned the uptick rule that short sales can only be instituted on an uptick. The lifting was based on studies that concluded that the uptick had had no effect (Bai 2007).

Short sales are criticized since they can create a downward spiral, a sort of negative bubble. But, that is just the opposite of an upward bubble, and it may serve to offset that. Realistically, there are opponents to allowing the practice of short selling because there are some with resources who naturally oppose them, namely the firms that are sold short. They are still banned in some countries, for a reason analogous to that which often explains why historically we have had so many tariffs: tariffs are lobbied for by industries that benefit from them, but the harm to the general public is widely dispersed and does not generate political action against tariffs.

Recent government efforts to intervene in the housing market, notably President Obama's Housing Affordability and Stability Plan, are justified as efforts to support the level of prices in housing markets, for a broader social purpose of maintaining prosperity. Sometimes these justifications are tempered with the qualification that the government should not try to maintain an artificially high level for home prices but should merely prevent home prices from "overshooting."

Any of these interventions in financial markets to encourage stability would have been unthinkable when the efficient markets hypothesis reigned supreme in academic settings. Now, these interventions are tolerated as exigencies, even though an academic theory that would justify them does not seem to be here yet.

The efficient markets hypothesis is one of the most remarkable errors in the history of thought, given its impact on our economic institutions and on the economy. Perhaps it is better to say that it is one of the most remarkable half-truths in the history of economic thought. Even Fama in 1970 recognized that there is some evidence against it. It is remarkable in the unfortunate tilt it has given to economic theorizing, and hence to countercyclical regulatory policy, that should have recognized what people were thinking and what was really happening.

Of course, the regulators can't accurately "time the market," but that does not mean that they should wash their hands completely of any thought of market bubbles that have psychological epidemics among their causes. The efficient markets theory has an essential contradiction in it, as noted long ago by Grossman and Stiglitz (1980): if everyone blankly assumes that the market is efficient, then they will not take action to exploit inefficiencies and so there will be no forces to make the market efficient. If everyone assumes the market is inefficient, and makes efforts to exploit this, then it will become efficient. With costly arbitrage, there is no rational expectations equilibrium. Perhaps, appending a little human psychology to their model, it is entirely to be expected that we may go between periods of belief in efficiency and periods of chastening.

One of the most important sources of human error noted by psychologists is inattention. The human mind, and human society, is very good at taking care of problems that they are focused on, but they can totally ignore problems until they get grotesquely out of hand. There is a social basis for attention, so even those Cassandras who try to point out problems as they are developing are often not listened to, not even heard. My take on this is that we need a systemic regulator whose charge is in part at least to try to think consistently about bubbles, even when others are looking elsewhere, and to take some, if limited, action against them as they are forming. We haven't had that recently because of the dominance of the efficient markets theory. We have to humanize policy regarding speculative bubbles and leverage, so that regulators' judgments based on their theory of mind can be applied.

Of course, taking judgmental actions against bubbles is not the only response to the leverage cycle. There are some technical fixes also needed, such as establishing clearinghouses for credit default swaps, which is already underway, adjusting macroprudential institutions that help eliminate the tendency for capital requirements to throttle lending in bad times (Turner Report 2009), and, as proposed by the Squam Lake Group, creating mechanisms for the creation of capital in bad times (French et al. 2010).

Encouraging Hedging Markets that Help Democratize Risk Management

As has been already noted, the current economic cycle is substantially caused by a failure to manage real estate risks, among both households and firms. Real estate risks directly impact most households, since most households are homeowners. Taking that as given, financial theory clearly asserts that individuals should take actions to hedge these risks.

Real estate risks are not easily managed because there are virtually no liquid markets for these risks. I and some of my colleagues have been trying for years to launch liquid markets for real estate risk, to provide an infrastructure for management of real estate risks. Doing this would be democratizing finance, since real estate risk is so important to the vast number of moderate income and lower income Americans.

In May, 2006, the Chicago Mercantile Exchange launched futures markets for single family homes in each of ten U.S. cities, and a futures market for the ten-city composite of these indexes. The market provides hedging opportunities. It also provides price discovery for the outlook for home prices going out five years. But unfortunately, as of this date, it has not taken off.

The hope when this market was launched was that it would be the basis for creation of new retail products that would democratize finance by addressing the real risks that homeowners face. It would make it possible for firms to offer such retail products as home equity insurance,[23] or equity sharing or co-ownership (Caplin et al. 1997), or continuous workout mortgages (Shiller 2003, 2008), and it might help facilitate the "prepackaged bankruptcy" plan proposed by Posner and Zingales (2009). Any of these might have prevented so many homeowners from getting into the situation that is now producing so many foreclosures.

It was hoped that the futures curve, which spelled out market expectations for the path of home prices for the succeeding five years, would help rationalize the business cycle. Soon after we launched our futures market in May 2006 it fell into strong backwardation, meaning the market was predicting massive declines in home prices in succeeding years. Of course, we do not believe that these markets are highly efficient, and the prices may not accurately forecast actual future price trends. However, it is noteworthy that the markets did forecast the extreme events in the housing market that produced the current financial crisis.

Had people been watching these markets, they would have seen the crisis coming, and presumably taking steps to prevent it. For example, builders may never have let the phenomenal housing construction boom, which peaked in 2006, continue, and so there would not be the huge inventory of unsold homes that is depressing the economy today.[24]

Promoting Other Technology for Democratizing Finance

The government has long had a role in financial innovation to serve the people better, and this fact should be remembered when we consider possible future innovations. The defined contribution pension fund is substantially encouraged and shaped by the Federal Government, through its tax policy (notably IRS Code 401(K) and 403(B)). The plans virtually did not exist before 1980. The real estate investment trust (REIT) was an invention of Congress in 1960, to allow small investors to participate in commercial real estate. It was an important step toward the democratization of finance. The mutual fund industry is essentially an invention of Congress (via the Investment Company Act of 1940) and regulators (via interpretations of the law that created the 401(k) plans in their present form) to help individuals manage their portfolios.

Consider the significance of this government-sponsored innovation, the mutual fund. Today, almost half of American households own mutual funds, directly or as part of a defined contribution pension plan. According to Flow of Funds Accounts of the Federal Reserve Table L122, there were $6.78 trillion of mutual fund shares outstanding in the second quarter of 2010 (down considerably from a high of $7.89 trillion in the third quarter of 2007 mostly because of declines in the market). This is a very substantial fraction of household

financial investments: by comparison, households directly
owned $5.50 trillion of equities and $3.88 trillion of credit market instruments, or $9.33 trillion total. This was an instance of
democratizing finance, by creating an ability for individuals
to own diversified portfolios of risky assets. But, these past innovations are not the end of the sequence of innovation. The
government should keep a role in future innovations as well.

Even the mutual fund industry stands to be improved.
The mutual fund industry is plagued by excessively high
fees and misleading advertising of the individual fund's ability to outperform the market. The high fees are substantially
encouraged, as Peter Wallison and Robert E. Litan argue, by
regulations that require that mutual funds each have a board
of directors who contract for an adviser to manage the fund,
and regulators expect the board to pay the adviser as a percentage of funds under management, allowing for a "reasonable profit," with "breakpoints" which cause the percentage
to decline as the fund grows larger. This structure inhibits
price competition between mutual funds, and encourages
large mutual fund families run by dominant securities firms.
They argue that the investment fund regulation should move
toward a model of Canada, Japan, and many countries of the
European Union: the regulatory structure should be changed
to allow advisers to compete directly with the public without the intervention of a board that is expected by regulators to enforce "reasonable profit."[25] Funds in these countries
do not have uniformly lower fees than in the U.S., but Wallison and Litan argue that there are other, separate, reasons
for this.

The misleading advertising of mutual fund industries has
the public largely convinced that they can successfully pick
dramatically winning mutual funds and that one ought to ex-

pect to pay high fees to winning fund managers. Mutual fund investors tend to move their funds toward the best performing firms (see for example Del Guercio and Tkac 2002). And yet past performance has been only a weak indicator of future returns (for example, see Berk and Green 2004). Tighter regulation of advertising should be reconsidered to help correct this egregious error.

Part of this misunderstanding by the public is encouraged by the structure of the fund industry in which the advertising of past returns, while controlled by regulators to be egregiously selective, remains misleading. Part of the problem has to do with the "incubator fund" problem. Mutual fund companies selectively advertise those of its funds that are successful, misleading individuals who do not understand that the companies have a deliberate policy of starting many "incubator" funds and then widely advertising those among them that chanced to be successful, eliminating the unsuccessful ones. To an investor unaware of this practice, reading the advertising seems to reveal evidence that a mutual fund is successful, and leads to a faulty impression of the persistence of returns to mutual fund management. The SEC has taken some enforcement actions against mutual fund companies that use the incubator fund strategy most aggressively and deceptively, particularly when the funds follow the strategy of allocating underpriced initial public offerings (IPOs) to such funds. But the basic problem remains rampant today (see Palmiter and Taha 2009). Regulation could inhibit the incubator fund practice, for example by requiring disclosure that reveals incubator fund status, or by prohibiting the use of incubator-period returns in advertising.

Beyond these steps, the government has a role in even broader measures to encourage the better management of individual-specific risks. One of the most salient facts about our risk management system is that many Americans (47 million in 2006, according to the Census Bureau) have not had health insurance at all. The Patient Protection and Affordable Care Act, signed into law by President Obama on March 30, 2010, was an example of significant government involvement in basic risk management. The Act creates new National Health Exchanges, creating new avenues for competition in providing low-cost health care, and limits insurance companies' latitude to charge higher premia for preexisting conditions, thereby making for more fundamental risk management.

Even beyond health insurance, there are other proposals yet to be fulfilled. There are proposals to extend unemployment insurance (Kippin 2009), and even to provide livelihood insurance against the vicissitudes of earning a living (Shiller 2003). There should even be infrastructure developments to facilitate these activities, such as the creation of a new system of economic units of measurement (Shiller 2009). If we are to really democratize finance, we need to consider all these broader avenues for the application of risk technology, with an inventiveness that takes account of the human barriers to the adoption of such innovations.

Investor Information

A more fundamental approach to many of these human problems would be to improve the state of investor information. Already, government regulation is heavily involved in promoting the availability and accuracy of investor information. For example, the SEC requires registration of financial advisors. In order to qualify, an advisor must pass Series 65 or 66 RIA Registered Investment Advisor Law exam administered under the auspices of the SRO FINRA. Similarly, the SEC requires the registration of stockbrokers. In order to qualify, the broker must pass Series 7 administered under the auspices of FINRA. But still the regulation is imperfect. These exams verify that the adviser or broker has basic knowledge of financial markets and of the laws regulating them. But the fact that they are licensed is misinterpreted by people as meaning that these people can be trusted. They often do not realize that their financial advisor is selling products to them, and often has little incentive to care about the product's real merits. The system has to be changed in ways that encourage more sense of fiduciary responsibility to clients than is the case at present.

President Obama's proposal for a new agency to protect individuals from bad financial practices, which was eventually enacted by Dodd-Frank with the Bureau of Consumer Financial Protection, will have the authority to collect information about financial practices and enact new rules to protect individuals against bad practices in credit cards, home mortgages, account overdrafts, payday loans, and other financial products.

The president's proposal drew on Elizabeth Warren's proposed "Financial Products Safety Commission," which would serve as an information center for financial abuses, much like the Consumer Products Safety Commission, which has been highly successful in protecting consumers against such things as dangerous cigarette lighters, cribs, and baby walkers. Her proposal is an analogous government agency to "collect data about which financial products are least understood, what kinds of disclosures are most effective, and which products are most likely to result in consumer default"—that is, to develop "expertise in consumer financial products."[26] Our financial regulators today have not been focused on the myriads of problems that consumers discover, another sign of our failure to implement objectives-based financial regulation.

The government already mandates extensive disclosure. William Brandeis, in his 1913 book *Other People's Money*, argued that disclosure should be central to regulatory policy, since, as he put it, "Sunshine is the best disinfectant." The SEC imposes an elaborate set of policies regarding prospectuses and free-writing prospectuses, when and how information can be distributed, when they can be shown at a meeting or road show, and when they must be filed electronically.

But, the effect of disclosure is often just to make it hard for investors to sue issuers afterwards. Most people do not really read these disclosures and rely instead on word of mouth, news media, and investment advisers for information (Shiller and Pound 1989). The disclosure is still a good thing, to the extent that these other sources digest what is in the disclosure. But the digestion of this information and its dissemination to ultimate investors is highly imperfect. As Elizabeth Warren has emphasized, one of the objectives of the agency she proposed would be to oversee how terms of consumer financial contracts are disclosed, questioning, for example, the 30-page credit card contracts, full of legalese designed to skirt consumer protection laws and class-action lawsuits. The disclosure must be effective for the people who need it.

The Squam Lake Group recommended (French et al. 2010) an expanded infrastructure specifically for systemically important institutions that would be designed to "bolster the government's ability to foresee, contain, and, ideally, prevent disruptions to the overall financial services industry." Creating databases will improve our understanding of systemic risks.

There has been a trend toward more timely reporting of market values. FAS 115, issued in 1993, was an important step, requiring that firms enter on their books the fair value of assets that are classified according to intent as trading securities or held-for-sale securities, though hold-to-maturity securities may be maintained in the books at their purchase price. There are some important behavioral questions about this. It may encourage short-term thinking. Benartzi and Thaler (1995) show that more frequent reporting encourages myopic loss aversion and causes lower prices.

Mark-to-market accounting is a sign of our information revolution, and so information is just more freely available. That is on balance a good thing. It is also a sign of faith in efficient markets. Many or most investment funds consider themselves to be in the business of producing alpha—of discovering assets that are underpriced or will perform better than the broad market expects. Asking them to perform mark-to-market accounting in times of economic stress amounts to asking them to deny the sales pitch that they have given their clients.

I have advocated (2008) the government's subsidizing of impartial, fee-only, dedicated financial advisors in such a way as to encourage their utilization by people at all income levels. "Fee-only" means that the advisors sign a statement that they will not take any compensation except the hourly fee from the client. "Dedicated" means that the financial advisor signs an oath of loyalty to the long-term interest of the client. What we want is someone who has an uncompromised relation with the client, and so is someone whom the client can reasonably trust for disinterested, and sympathetic, advice.

The U.S. government already subsidizes financial advice, since it is deductible under Form 1040, Miscellaneous Expenses, Schedule A, "Job Expenses and Certain Miscellaneous Deductions," line 23, of the Federal Income Tax. But it is deductible only for those who itemize, and only to the extent that miscellaneous expenses exceed two percent of adjusted gross income. It therefore excludes people of modest incomes, and of course the extent of the subsidy is also low for those people who are in lower income tax brackets. My proposal is that the government should give a more uniform subsidy to advisors who sign a statement that they are fee-only and are dedicated to the clients, much like the statement that the National Association of Personal Financial Advisors demands of its members.

The SEC restricts the sale of sophisticated investments such as hedge funds to investors who are "accredited investors" as defined in SEC Regulation D. Accredited investors must have either high income or high wealth. The accredited investor definition provided by the SEC may no longer survive in the new world of democratized finance that the public will demand in response to the present crisis. The present accredited investor rules have in fact been circumvented anyway by funds of funds, who invest in accredited-investor-only securities on behalf of smaller investors, but who sometimes multiply the fees exorbitantly and do not attend to the economic situation of the investor as an advisor would. Recent proposals have been made to modify the wealth and income requirements for accredited investor status. For example, Finger (2009) proposes that individuals of modest wealth and income be offered an alternative route to accredited investor status, passing a licensing exam.

Subsidizing financial advisors for everyone and eliminating the wealth and income requirements for accredited investor status would be major steps toward democratizing finance, and toward helping to establish an improved sense of fairness and basic justice in our financial system.

Conclusion

The new facilities and government agencies that have already been created in reaction to the economic crisis that began in 2007 can, if they are managed well, dramatically improve our financial markets. If they are managed poorly, they could stifle innovation and entrepreneurship and inhibit economic success. The overriding question that remains before us is how these beginnings should lead to a stronger and more effective form of capitalism in the future.

I have argued here that future government regulatory actions by government agencies, including the new ones created by Dodd-Frank, as well as rule-setting actions of SROs, industry groups, and individual businesses, should be aimed at exploiting important opportunities for democratizing and humanizing finance. The reforms we have seen to date should be considered only the beginning, only setting the stage for the real reforms to come. The people who run government regulatory agencies or SROs will have to decide what, within their mandate, they will do that is fundamentally different from the practices that brought us the current crisis. There are fundamental problems to tackle: how we deal with financial crises and their complex roots in psychological feedback and procyclical saving behavior, employment and risk management policies, and promoting consumer protection in such a way as to allow individuals to take best advantage of the possibilities of risk management. Both democratizing and humanizing finance can be enhanced only if those responsible for regulation think creatively about how to better involve people in a healthy and vibrant financial system. It is about getting rid of the arbitrariness and strict rules orientation of the regulatory framework that has left us with regulators who themselves often cannot make good sense of the charges they are left with.

As noted above, Dodd-Frank has fulfilled the Obama Administration's request for a new Financial Services Oversight Council, that would "identify emerging risks" like those that led to the current crisis.[27] The Council will have to pay some greater attention to identifying emerging risks. And yet Dodd-Frank itself does not give a method of achieving this. The Act does not say how bubbles can be recognized and dealt with. Humanizing finance means paying attention to the human element of economic crises, and to the emerging field of behavioral economics, which until recently has had little impact on government policy. Regulators have to be people who appreciate the revolution that is going on in economics. Its ultimate success with the regulatory reform depends on its continued willingness to do stay up to date.

The Obama Treasury Department's proposal for a consumer financial protection agency said it would, among other things, "be authorized to provide standards for 'plain vanilla' products that are simpler and have straightforward pricing."[28] This recommendation appears to be motivated by some recent research in behavioral finance that shows how difficult it is for people to choose among complex financial products.[29] Although Dodd-Frank makes no reference to the term "plain vanilla," it does say that the Bureau of Consumer Financial Protection will assure that "markets for consumer financial products and services operate transparently and efficiently."[30] Creating plain vanilla products and assuring transparency is an example of humanizing finance, taking account of human foibles that prevent people from reading long prospectuses and doing complex weighing of factors. At the same time, however, we do not want plain vanilla to mean old-fashioned. The old-fashioned conventional mortgage, combined with high leverage and a volatile housing market, has wiped out the life savings of millions of people. Recommending plain vanilla products should also be an opportunity to create new standards for products, so that they function even better. That is what the Roosevelt Administration's Home Owners Loan Corporation achieved in 1933 when it made the long-term mortgage a new standard—a sensible redefinition of plain vanilla mortgage that was a distinct improvement on the older short-term mortgage. We have to update the Roosevelt standard again today. Analogous new steps might be government sponsorship of "plain vanilla" products like home equity insurance, home equity sharing, continuous workout mortgages, or prepackaged homeowners' bankruptcy plans. The adoption of such relatively plain vanilla products could be enhanced by subsidizing financial advice for everyone. Such new steps should be transformational elements in democratizing finance that will create a better capitalist economy. We must avoid appointing plain vanilla people who do not understand financial innovation to run the Bureau of Consumer Financial Protection or we will stop progress.

Democratizing finance means focusing on creatively extending the capitalist principles of risk management so that they really work for everyone. It means an adventure in financial innovation, with a lot of new ideas considered, and some amount of experimentation and risk taking.

The human tragedy of the current financial crisis has forced us into an embarrassing sequence of bailouts and special favors, which offend the notions of order and fairness. But the human tragedy need not have been dealt with in such terms, if we had planned from the outset on how to deal with such things: that would be risk management rather than bailout. We need to think instead about extending risk management to the people. This process requires some careful financial engineering. The examples given here are only beginnings. Making this happen will take years of effort, but, then again, we may be living with this financial crisis for many more years.

Humanizing finance means really incorporating the knowledge being provided to us by the various branches of cognitive science into a plan for improved human-factors financial engineering. The examples given here of such advances are at best only a beginning. The twenty-first century is likely to be a time of rapid development of our understanding of the human mind and its interfaces with information technology. We have to see that all of our improved knowledge is implemented into a better financial system.

The current financial crisis will be forgotten some day. What is most important is the opportunity it has given us to focus our attentions on bringing our financial system up to date, and the new rules of operation that will be with us for many years to come.

Notes

An earlier version of this paper was presented at the Alvin Hansen Symposium Series on Public Policy, *Reregulating the U.S. Financial Markets: What to Do Once the Crisis Is Over*, April 30, 2009, including also Randall S. Kroszner, discussants Benjamin M. Friedman, George G. Kaufman, Robert C. Pozen, and Hal S. Scott.

1. The conference version of this paper, upon which the comments in this volume are based, preceded the announcement of the Obama Administration's June 2009 plan and the July 2010 Dodd-Frank Wall Street Reform and Consumer Protection Act.

2. U.S. Treasury (2009), p. 4.

3. Treasury Secretary Tim Geithner, Written Testimony House Financial Services Committee Hearing, March 26, 2009.

4. *American Heritage Dictionary of the English Language*, Boston: Houghton-Mifflin, 1996, pp. 2090–2121.

5. Jonathan Miller, of the appraisal firm Miller Samuels, wrote to me in 2008 that "AMCs should be vested in the exposure of the transaction. In other words, when a mortgage loan is sold off and goes sour, they need to be incentivized to promote appraisal quality—otherwise this whole effort is meaningless." Moreover, "All appraisals, or automated value products must be furnished to the borrower. Common practice is that lenders keep ordering AVMs or appraisals until a high enough report comes to make the deal."

6. Paulson, Nason, and Steele (2008).

7. U.S. Treasury (2009), p. 3.

8. Dodd-Frank Wall Street Reform and Consumer Protection Act, 2010, §113 (a) (1) p 23. http://frwebgate.access.gpo.gov/cgi-bin/getdoc.cgi?dbname =111_cong_bills&docid=f:h4173enr.txt.pdf.

9. Dodd-Frank, 2010, §165 (a) (1) (A) pp. 48–49. http://frwebgate.access.gpo .gov/cgi-bin/getdoc.cgi?dbname=111_cong_bills&docid=f:h4173enr.txt.pdf.

10. See Coats et al. (2009).

11. Sylvia F. Porter, "Lessons for '49 in the Crash of '29" New York Times, Oct 23, 1949, p. SM13.

12. In partial response to this sense of unfairness, the U.S. Treasury encouraged several large investment companies to create "bailout funds," which would allow retail investors to participate in the government bailouts to financial institutions as investors. Of course, people could participate in the bailouts in many ways, by investing in companies that participate in them, but a more direct participation was apparently seen as symbolic.

13. U.S. Treasury (2009), p. 39.

14. The need for SEC disclosure rules can be justified in terms of various principles of behavioral economics: overconfidence, illusion of control, self-serving biases, and ambiguity aversion. See Langevoort (2000).

15. Richard Brealey and Stewart Myers, Principles of Corporate Finance, 2nd Edition, McGraw Hill, 1984, p. 784.

16. Richard Brealey, Steward Myers, and Franklin Allen, Principles of Corporate Finance, 9th Edition, McGraw Hill, 2008, p. 972.

17. Economist Scott Sumner, in a quotation described as "great stuff" by Greg Mankiw on his blog on March 22, 2009, put it this way: "So the anti-EMH argument for regulation must be based on the following; bankers are irrational and make lots of foolish loans. Regulators are rational and can see that these loans are too risky, and can protect bankers from hurting themselves. At a theoretical level this doesn't even pass the laugh test."

18. Wolk and Nikolai (1997), p. 11.

19. Quoted in The Origin of Financial Crises by George Cooper.

20. Scott (2005), p. 4.

21. Interestingly, the same volume edited by Scott has an important paper by Mark Flannery (2005) about systemic risk management using reverse convertible debentures, an idea that was developed further by the Squam

Lake Group (French et al., 2010) and has been renamed regulatory hybrid securities.

22. "The New Margin Requirements," *Hartford Courant*, October 29, 1937, p. 16.

23. Home equity insurance dates back to Oak Park Illinois in 1977. I and my colleagues have been arguing over the years for such innovations, and that settlement of claims might best be in terms of home price indexes that are also traded on derivatives markets, so that the risks can be hedged (Shiller 1993). In 2009, Representative Barnie Frank began drafting legislation to make home equity insurance a reality.

24. MacroMarkets LLC made an effort to auction MacroShares Major Metro Housing, real estate securities that traded on NYSE/Arca and were based on the S&P/Case-Shiller Home Price Indices. These five-year securities, with ticker symbols UMM (for up major metro) and DMM (for down major metro), traded with the ease of stocks and allowed long or short positions in single family homes. These, if they had succeeded, would have produced greater price discovery and also stimulated more liquidity in the futures market for home prices.

25. Wallison and Litan (2007).

26. Warren (2007).

27. U.S. Treasury (2009), p. 10.

28. U.S. Treasury (2009), p. 15.

29. Benartzi and Thaler (2002).

30. Dodd-Frank, 2010, §1021 (b) (5), p. 605. http://frwebgate.access.gpo .gov/cgi-bin/getdoc.cgi?dbname=111_cong_bills&docid=f:h4173enr.txt.pdf.

References

Akerlof, George A., and Robert J. Shiller. 2009. *Animal Spirits: How Human Psychology Drives the Economy and Why It Matters for Global Capitalism*. Princeton: Princeton University Press.

Bai, Lynn. 2007. "The Uptick Rule of Short Sale Regulation—Can It Alleviate Downward Pressure from Negative Earnings Shocks?" Unpublished paper. University of Cincinnati College of Law.

Benartzi, Shlomo, and Richard H. Thaler. 1995. Myopic Loss Aversion and the Equity Premium Puzzle. *Quarterly Journal of Economics* 110 (1) (February):73–92.

Benartzi, Shlomo, and Richard H. Thaler. 2002. How Much Is Investor Autonomy Worth? *Journal of Finance* 57 (4) (August):1593–1616.

Berk, Jonathan, and Richard C. Green. 2004. Mutual Fund Flows and Performance in Rational Markets. *Journal of Political Economy* 112:1269.

Brandeis, Louis D. 1913. *Other People's Money and How the Bankers Use It.* New York: F.A. Stokes.

Caplin, Andrew, Sewin Chan, Charles Freeman, and Joseph Tracy. 1997. *Housing Partnerships: A New Approach to a Market at a Crossroads.* Cambridge, M.A.: MIT Press.

Coats, David, Will Hutton, and Matteo Razzanelli. 2009. *Tackling the Global Jobs Crisis: Why the G20 Summit Matters.* London: The Work Foundation.

Del Guercio, Diane, and Paula A. Tkac. 2002. The Determinants of the Flow of Funds of Managed Portfolios: Mutual Funds v. Pension Funds., *Journal of Finance and Quantitative Analysis* 37:523–533.

Fama, Eugene. 1970. Efficient Markets: A Review of Theory and Empirical Work. *Journal of Finance* 25 (2):383–417.

Finger, Wallis K. 2009. Unsophisticated Wealth: Reconsidering the SEC's "Accredited Investor" Definition Under the 1933 Act. *Washington University Law Review* 86(3):733–767. http://lawreview.wustl.edu/in-print /unsophisticated-wealth-reconsidering-the-sec%E2%80%99s-%E2%80%9C accredited-investor%E2%80%9D-definition-under-the-1933-act/.

Flannery, Mark. 2005. No Pain, No Gain? Effecting Market Discipline via "Reverse Convertible Debentures." In *Capital Adequacy beyond Basel: Banking, Securities, and Insurance,* ed. Hal Scott. New York: Oxford University Press, 171–196.

Fostel, Ana, and John Geanakoplos. 2008. Leverage Cycles and the Anxious Economy. *American Economic Review* 98 (4)(September):1211–1244.

French, Kenneth, et al. 2010. *The Squam Lake Report: Fixing the Financial System.* Princeton: Princeton University Press.

Friedman, Milton. 1962. *Capitalism and Freedom.* Chicago: University of Chicago Press.

Friedman, Milton and Anna J. Schwartz. 1963. *A Monetary History of the United States 1867-1960*. Princeton: Princeton University Press.

Goldberg, Michael, and Roman Frydman. 2009. "Financial Markets and the State: Price Swings, Risk, and the Scope of Regulation." Presented at Center for Capitalism and Society conference.

Gramlich, Edward. 2007. *Subprime Mortgages: America's Latest Boom and Bust*. Washington, D.C.: Urban Institute Press.

Grossman, Sanford, and Joseph Stiglitz. 1980. On the Impossibility of Informationally Efficient Markets. *American Economic Review* 70 (3):393–408.

Kahneman, Daniel, Jack Knetsch, and Richard Thaler. 1986. Fairness as a Constraint on Profit Seeking: Entitlements in the Market. *American Economic Review* 76 (4).

Kashyap, Anil, Raghuram Rajan, and Jeremy Stein. 2008. "Rethinking Capital Regulation," Jackson Hole Symposium.

Kippin, Henry. 2009. *Anglo-Flexicurity: Insuring against Unemployment in the UK*. London: The Social Market Foundation.

Langevoort, Donald C. 2000. Organized Illusions: A Behavioral Theory of Why Corporations Mislead Stock Market Investors (and Cause Other Social Harms). In *Behavioral Law and Economics*, ed. Cass Sunstein and Richard Thaler. Cambridge, U.K.: Cambridge University Press, 144–167.

Palmiter, Alan, and Ahmed Taha. 2009. Star Creation: The Manipulation of Mutual Fund Performance through Incubation. *Vanderbilt Law Review* 62 (5):1485–1534.

Paulson, Henry M., Richard K. Steel, and David Nason. 2008. *Blueprint for a Modernized Financial Regulatory Structure*, Washington D.C.: U.S. Treasury.

Polanyi, Karl. 1944. *The Great Transformation*. New York: Rinehart.

Posner, Eric A., and Luigi Zingales. 2009. "The Housing Crisis and Bankruptcy Reform: The Prepackaged Chapter 13 Approach." Unpublished paper. University of Chicago. April.

Pozen, Robert. 2010. *Too Big to Save? How to Fix the Financial System*. New York: John Wiley.

Rajan, Raghuram. 2005. "Has Financial Development Made the World Riskier?" Federal Reserve Bank of Kansas City: Jackson Hole Symposium. August.

Scott, Hal S. 2005. *Capital Adequacy beyond Basel: Banking, Securities, and Insurance.* New York: Oxford University Press.

Shiller, Robert J. 1993. *Macro Markets: Creating New Institutions for Managing Society's Largest Economic Risks.* Oxford: Oxford University Press.

Shiller, Robert J. 2003. *The New Financial Order.* Princeton: Princeton University Press.

Shiller, Robert J. 2005. *Irrational Exuberance.* 2nd ed. Princeton: Princeton University Press.

Shiller, Robert J. 2008. *Subprime Solution: How Today's Global Financial Crisis Happened and What to Do about It.* Princeton: Princeton University Press.

Shiller, Robert J. 2009. *The Case for a Basket: A New Way of Showing the True Value of Money.* With the assistance of Lawrence Kay. London: The Policy Exchange.

Shiller, Robert J., and John Pound. 1989. Survey Evidence on the Diffusion of Interest and Information among Investors. *Journal of Economic Behavior & Organization* 12:47–66.

Shin, Hyun Song. 2008. "Risk and Liquidity in a System Context." Presented at Bank for International Settlements Conference.

Shin, Hyung Song. 2009. Reflections on Northern Rock: The Bank Run that Heralded the Global Financial Crisis. *Journal of Economic Perspectives* 23 (1):101–119.

Turner, Adair. March 2009. *The Turner Review: A Regulatory Response to the Global Banking Crisis.* London: Financial Services Authority.

U.S. Treasury. 2009. *Financial Regulatory Reform: A New Foundation; Rebuilding Financial Supervision and Regulation.* Washington, D.C. June.

Wallison, Peter J., and Robert E. Litan. 2007. *Competitive Equity: A Better Way to Organize Mutual Funds.* Washington, D.C.: The AEI Press.

Warren, Elizabeth. 2007. Unsafe at Any Rate. *Democracy* 5. Summer. http://www.democracyjournal.org/article2.php?ID=6528&limit=0&limit2=1500&page=1.

Wolk, Carel, and Loren A. Nikolai. 1997. Personality Types of Accounting Students and Faculty: Comparisons and Implications. *Journal of Accounting Education* 15 (1):1–17.

2 Making Markets More Robust

Randall S. Kroszner

We have experienced the most severe global financial crisis since the Great Depression. The sharp, synchronized falloff of real economic activity that occurred in the fall of 2008 is unprecedented. Reform of regulatory policies and of market practices are necessary to reduce the likelihood of such events. While we are still learning lessons from this crisis, I will suggest some paths for reform that can help to make markets more robust going forward.

The goal of such reforms would be to support sustainable long run economic growth, consistent with solid and sensible protection of consumers. Reforms should focus on reducing the likelihood that a ripple caused by trouble at or failure of one institution turns into a tidal wave that can affect the financial system and the economy more broadly—the classic systemic risk problem. To mitigate systemic risk in the system, reducing procyclicality of regulation and market practices is a high priority.

Squarely facing and mitigating "too big to fail" and "too interconnected to fail" problems is another important theme. The "too big" and "too interconnected" problems arise from weaknesses in the market and legal infrastructure, for instance, inefficiencies and uncertainties in bankruptcy codes and procedures that can lead creditors, customers, and counterparties to "run" on an institution, as I will describe below. Another key theme is that the "originate to distribute" model and securitization put heavy requirements on the market and legal infrastructure. Ensuring accurate and timely information is available to market participants and supervisors is crucial for avoiding concentrations of risk and the loss of confidence that comes when there is not sufficient information about particular securities or institutions to assess those risks. Sensible protections of consumers can not only help to reduce harm to consumers but also avoid uncertainty about underwriting standards and performance of, for example, mortgages included in securitizations that have shaken the confidence in the securitization process itself.

Given that the Financial Stability Board (FSB)—an international body comprised of officials from finance ministries, central banks, and financial supervisors—has proposed more than sixty different reforms to the G-20, my remarks here will be far from comprehensive (FSB 2009). I will, for example, not touch on important accounting issues. In addition, rather than go into detail on proposals for reducing the procyclical elements of capital regulations, loan loss provisioning, and leverage, I will recommend the recent FSB report on these matters (FSB 2008).

Instead, I will highlight a few key aspects of the current reform discussion related to market and legal infrastructure, "too big" and "too interconnected" to fail, and the procyclicality of some market practices. I emphasize these issues because I believe that they are crucial to begin to address fragilities of the financial system revealed by the events of the last few years.

Much has been written—and will continue to be written—on the causes and origins of the crisis (a selective and very far from comprehensive list would include Adrian and Shin 2009, Brunnermeier 2009, Diamond and Rajan 2009, Friedman 2009, Gorton 2009, Kroszner 2008a and 2008b, Kroszner and Melick forthcoming, Posner 2009, Rajan 2009, and Shin 2008 and 2009). Rather than delve deeply into that subject, I begin in the next section with an extremely brief overview of my perspective on some key vulnerabilities that the current crisis has revealed. The subsequent sections then focus upon five areas of reform that I believe are necessary to improve information and incentives for private market actors and government supervisors in order to make the financial system more robust going forward.

First is the role that credit rating agencies play in the informational infrastructure. I will argue that we should not throw the baby out with the bathwater since ratings in traditional corporate debt area, in contrast to structured/securitized products, have continued to be reasonably reliable proxies for risk. Second, I will discuss reforms of the mortgage securitization market, including the role of consumer protection and information provision, which will be crucial to revive that important source of financing.

Third, I will turn to the problems of instability and "funding runs" that arise by not having a robust framework for resolving nonbank financial institutions. Fourth, I will argue that moving over-the-counter derivative contracts to platforms with central counterparty clearing will be crucial to making markets more robust. Reforming the resolution regime and the over-the-counter (OTC) market will help to make institutions less interconnected and the system less vulnerable to ripples from a failure becoming a tidal wave. I will then end with a brief discussion of provisions in some contracts that might at first appear to protect counterparties but can be destabilizing to the market as a whole.

The 2010 Dodd-Frank Wall Street Reform and Consumer Protection Act, passed after the original draft of this paper was presented at the Alvin Hansen Symposium at Harvard, touches on all but the last of the five areas of reform I focus on here. Whether the Act will ultimately be successful in addressing these issues, however, will depend crucially on how it is implemented since the Act leaves so many significant decisions to subsequent regulatory rule-making and supervisory action. I hope my suggestions for reform can provide useful guidance in the effective implementation of the Act as well as highlight areas for reform beyond Dodd-Frank.

Key Vulnerabilities of the Financial System

Since the last major round of regulatory reform in the 1930s, financial intermediation has grown much more complicated and interconnected but the regulatory framework has not kept pace. Much of the regulatory structure has focused on protecting banks and what had been their primary source of finance, that is, deposits. But banks do not play the same role they once did and the fragilities are not the same as they were when much of the structure of oversight was created. Sixty years ago, for example, depository institutions held roughly 60 percent of the assets in the financial sector but by 2006 that share fell in half to 30 percent (see Kroszner and Melick forthcoming).

Transformations have occurred on both the liability and asset sides of the balance sheets that have created greater interlinkages. Deposits have become a less important source of funding. Banks, as well as other financial institutions, increasingly have come to rely on market-based sources of short-term funding, such as commercial paper, asset-backed commercial paper, and the repurchase agreement market. Money Market Mutual Funds, which didn't exist before the 1970s but now hold roughly $4 trillion of assets (roughly half the size of bank deposits), have become key sources of this funding. Instability in money market funds, for example, can have enormous consequences for the rest of the system.

On the asset side, banks and other intermediaries had come to rely increasingly on the ability to securitize, that is, sell, assets they generate, that is, loans and mortgages. This "originate to distribute" model of intermediation thus relies heavily on the operation of the securitization markets, thereby making the intermediaries more vulnerable to any instabilities that arise in these markets.

With these transformations, the banking and intermediation system more generally has come to be characterized by long chains with many of the crucial links in the chain being market-based, nonbank intermediaries that do not rely on deposits for their funding (see Adrian and Shin 2009, Kroszner 2010, and Kroszner and Melick forthcoming). The many layers of intermediation in the modern financial system thus create chains of inter-linkages that can make the system more vulnerable to shocks in any one single market or institution. Mismanagement or misjudgments about risk in particular institutions or markets, rather than self-correcting through the elimination of players who made the mistakes, can cascade through the system and raise questions about the viability of institutions throughout the system. A market-wide breakdown of confidence can then occur due to the potential inter-linkages and lack of knowledge of the counterparty exposures and uncertainty about whether those counterparties will be able to make good on their contractual promises when they are experiencing stress. Previously deep and liquid markets can suddenly freeze, revealing the high reliance on leverage and, in particular, on the short-term funding of longer-term assets such as mortgages.

The increased reliance on the smooth functioning of markets affecting both the liability and asset sides of the balance sheet also puts an increasing burden on the resiliency of the infrastructure of those markets, particularly on information and on legal aspects of contract clarity and enforcement. As I describe in the following sections, a number of reforms can help to make these chains of intermediation less vulnerable to any individual weak link in that long and complex chain.

Role of Credit Ratings and Credit Rating Agencies: Don't Throw the Baby Out with the Bathwater

Much of the public and private supervisory system relies, at least in part, upon assessments made by the large credit ratings agencies, e.g., Moody's, Standard & Poor's, and Fitch, as well as a number of smaller or more specialized organizations. These ratings constitute an important part of the informational infrastructure that takes on particular importance in financial systems relying heavily upon market-based financing rather than traditional deposits.

On the public side, capital charges for some classes of securities, derivatives, and loans are adjusted to take into account the credit rating of a borrower or counterparty. The Securities and Exchange Commission (SEC) has long given preferential treatment in terms of lower capital requirements or "haircuts" for highly rated securities. Bank supervisors around the world have incorporated ratings into their assessments of capital adequacy, and the Basel II capital framework gives concrete guidelines on how ratings should affect capital for certain types of assets. Ratings also are used to restrict what may be held in certain portfolios. Rule 2a-7 under the Investment Company Act of 1940, for example, prohibited money market funds from holding short-term debt securities that are below certain top ratings categories. (See SEC 2005.) The Dodd-Frank Act as well as recent regulatory actions, however, are helping to reduce the reliance on credit ratings on the public side.

Private actors also rely on credit ratings in a variety of ways. Many internal risk management systems and investment committee guidelines at institutional investors, for example, rely heavily on ratings to determine portfolio allocation and what can and cannot be held in portfolio. Downgrades, in some cases, can lead to a requirement by a portfolio manager to sell particular securities. As I will discuss in the final section on potentially destabilizing contracts, a rating downgrade is used in many contracts as a trigger to require restrictions on activities, to post additional capital, or to take other steps to provide added protection for the counterparty.

In principle, credit ratings can be an efficient way to summarize the rich and complex information known about a firm or security, and that is why they have become so widely used by supervisors and in private markets. When John Moody first proposed some form of simple ratings scale just prior to WWI, many in the markets ridiculed him for trying to do the impossible. By the 1920s, however, simple rating scales had become commonplace and their importance was recognized by the SEC in the 1930s. The development of ratings scales that allow for easy comparisons of different securities parallels the development of consistent grading systems for grains and other commodities developed on the many commodities and futures exchanges during the nineteenth and twentieth centuries, which allowed those markets to become more liquid (see Kroszner 1999).

Over time, both through SEC rules and private choices, there has been increasing reliance on the ratings issued by the Nationally Recognized Statistical Ratings Organizations

(NRSROs, a term coined in 1975), which are regulated by the SEC. Part of this increasing reliance had come from a lengthening track record where, at least in the realm of traditional corporate debt, the ratings were seen to be reasonably reliable proxies of risk. The spectacular failure to provide reliable guidance about the risks in structured financial products, particularly mortgage-backed securities (MBS) and collateralized debt obligations (CDO), in the last few years, however, has led to calls for major reforms (e.g., FSB 2009). These proposals range from greater transparency in the ratings process to fundamental changes in the business model and even government-run ratings organizations.

Let's make sure, however, that we do not throw out the baby with the bathwater. A major focus of concern has been the potential for conflict of interest when the firms or creators of the securities to be rated are those who pay the rating agencies. It is important to remember that this has been the business model of rating agencies for decades. Although the potential for conflict has long been there, why did the rating agencies not succumb earlier? Why have the credit ratings on traditional corporate debt performed reasonably well through this severe downturn, in stark contrast to those on structured products, since the same potential conflict "to please the issuer" would exist for both traditional corporate debt and structured products?

I believe that competition, or the lack of it, can explain the difference. With traditional corporate debt, there are many analysts who follow individual companies and provide their own assessments of a firm's prospects and risks. They are able to do so because a substantial amount of publicly disclosed data is readily available, so the "information advantage" that a credit rating agency might have compared to an industry analyst may not be great. In addition, the models for assessing risks in corporate debt are relatively well established, and long histories of data exist to test and stress models in a variety of economic conditions. Thus, although there are only three large rating agencies, they effectively face significant competition from a large number of industry analysts and market participants who, at relatively low cost, can undertake their own due diligence. In other words, "trust but verify" can operate reasonably effectively in these markets.

Contrast this situation with structured credit products, such as tranches of MBS and CDOs (see Kroszner 2008c). First, they are relatively new instruments with relatively short histories, particularly under stress situations. Second, the securities tend to be more complex and difficult to model, requiring much more specialized knowledge than typical corporate debt would. Third, the MBS and CDO securities were not standardized. Not only were the protocols for loss sharing among the "tranches" of the securities (so-called "waterfall") different across issues, but the circumstances under which the mortgage services were or were not permitted to restructure mortgages also varied considerably. Fourth, there was no standardization of data about the characteristics of the assets going into these securities, once again making it costly for outsiders to undertake their own assessment of risk. Fifth, most of these securities were relatively small issues so there were higher costs, relatively to the issue size, to determine and assess the unique features of each MBS or CDO issue. (I will analyze problems that these characteristics pose for the revival of securitization in the next section.)

Thus, the ratings agencies effectively faced significantly less competition in their assessment of structured products than in traditional corporate debt.[1] The different behavior of the credit rating agencies in the two realms is illustrated by the following: at the start of 2008, a dozen firms received a triple-A rating but more than 64,000 structured financial products received the coveted triple-A rating (Blankfein 2009). I believe that competition differences are fundamental to understanding the continued reliability of credit ratings in areas such as corporate debt while simultaneously ratings for structured products have proved to be distressingly unreliable.

Introducing more competition, directly or indirectly, should be the focus of reforms for credit rating agencies. The Dodd-Frank Act and actions of the SEC will improve codes of conduct and increase the transparency of how the models and data are used by the ratings agencies. While these changes will be helpful for allowing greater monitoring of the agencies by market participants, they are only small steps in the direction of enhancing effective competition that the rating agencies are working toward. There is continuing debate in the U.S. and in a number of G-20 countries on whether there should be more fundamental reforms about the rating agency model, including amendments to Dodd-Frank that ultimately were not included in the final legislation. In particular, some have suggested that ending the "issuer pays" model and requiring an "investor pays" model would address the problem. Although I think it is important to allow different business models to compete and that barriers to entry into the ratings business should be reduced, I think that when there is sufficient competition, ratings produced under the traditional business model can be reliable. Also, there is a potential for conflict of interest on the part of some classes of investors, who might like to achieve higher rates of return but still satisfy regulatory or contractual requirements restricting investments to highly rated instruments. They might have an incentive for "grade inflation." (See Calomiris 2009.) Thus, an "investor pays" model will not necessarily produce superior outcomes and runs the risk of throwing the baby out with the bathwater.

As I will argue in the next section, for the securitization markets to revive, fundamental changes need to take place in market practices that would allow for lower costs for investors to undertake their own due diligence and, thus, effectively increase the competition and scrutiny that rating agencies face in this realm.

Reviving the Securitization Markets and the Role of Consumer Protection

In principle, mortgage securitizations make good economic sense: by providing access to the broad capital market, securitization allows loan originators to access a wider source of funding than they can obtain directly. In addition, securitization can limit an originator's exposure to prepayment risks associated with interest rate movements, to geographic concentrations of loans, and to credit and funding risks associated with holding mortgages all the way to maturity. Effectively, securitization can significantly lower the cost of extending home loans, and lower costs can be passed along to homeowners in the form of lower mortgage rates.

The housing government-sponsored enterprises (GSEs— Freddie Mac and Fannie Mae, also called "agencies") have played an important role in the development of mortgage securitization in the United States. In large part, the broad appeal of agency MBS can be traced to the explicit guarantee of the securities by the sponsoring agencies. There also was a perception fostered by the agencies themselves of implicit government backing. The GSE guarantees implied that the returns to investors of undertaking a thorough and costly credit analysis of underlying mortgages in agency MBS pools were low, so that task was essentially left to the agencies themselves. The GSEs took on increasing risks without managing those risks effectively, particularly as their activities and balance sheet expanded rapidly.

Obviously, the result has not been salutary for the GSEs, the mortgage market, or the taxpayer. Even as agency MBS issuance took off in the 1970s and 1980s, the most basic infrastructure needed to conduct credit analysis on home mortgage pools—comprehensive loan-level data that was broadly accessible in a standardized format—went essentially undeveloped. Private market participants had little incentive to undertake the costly task of building databases and monitoring the individual loans, given the insurance from the GSEs that was perceived to be ultimately backed by the U.S. Treasury. The GSEs, of course, did not have an incentive to provide information to the market since they emphasized the implicit government guarantee. Providing more data would have helped to foster the development of mortgage-modeling by potential competitors to the GSEs. Thus, the encouragement of the growth of the MBS market through the GSE activities, with their implicit government guarantees, came at the price of reduced market monitoring and underdevelopment of the informational infrastructure.

During the early- to mid-2000s, potential competitors to the GSEs began to issue "private-label" MBS (that is, not issued by the GSEs) in increasing volume but the data and information infrastructure was lagging behind. The paucity and inaccessibility of data about the underlying home loans was a contributing factor to why private-label MBS was able to expand so rapidly in 2005 through early 2007 despite a deterioration in underwriting standards and prospective credit performance. That is not to say that better data would necessarily have led investors to anticipate the problems in private-label MBS. But I do think it was a significant hindrance that the information needed to infer, in real time, the extent to which subprime and alt-A mortgage underwriting standards were sliding simply did not exist in a form that allowed the widespread scrutiny or objective analyses needed to bring these risks more clearly into focus.

Ironically, the "tranching" or slicing up of the payment streams of the private-label MBS was partially in response to demand for greater protection for purchasers of the private-label MBS due to the lack of GSE guarantees. As with any rapidly developing market, there is a learning process during which it takes time to understand risks and stress-test models. Market participants initially relied heavily upon the credit rating agencies to do analysis and provide the imprimatur of a AAA-rating because the development of the infrastructure for doing private due diligence in this market had been slowed by the role of the GSEs and the perception of government guarantees.

The tranches often involved payoff structures that included sharp "cliff effects" or "tail risks" that were difficult to model and evaluate; in other words, the potential to deviate from "average performance" was difficult to know. These structures were very different than those of traditional debt securities that the credit rating agencies had been evaluating for many years. The low-probability "tail risks" thus did not receive sufficient scrutiny in a market where it was particularly difficult to undertake independent due diligence, that is, to trust but verify (see Kroszner 2008d).

While comprehensive loan-level data for mortgage pools are necessary to rebuild confidence in private-label MBS (and the American Securitization Forum is undertaking such a project[2]), improvements in the contractual structure of private-label MBS are also needed to revive the market and address some of the sources of the failure of the credit rating agencies in this market, as noted in the previous section.

First, in recent years, the complexity of many deals made non-agency MBS difficult to value. For example, looking at private-label MBS deals constructed in the heyday of 2006, some subprime trusts included three separate pools of mortgages—for example, prime-rated jumbo loans, alt-A first liens, and a blend of subprime first and junior liens—with cash flows that were prioritized using complicated payoff rules among more than a dozen different securities. The securitization contract might have dictated that one AAA-rated tranche be paid using cash flows only from the prime jumbo loans, while another AAA-rated tranche could have received no payments at all from that pool. Given that future investors will rely less on the credit rating and will wish to be able to do their own due diligence, simpler structures that are more standardized and easier to evaluate will be necessary to bring down information costs in this market.

Second, fewer and larger tranches in private-label MBS could have a couple of key benefits. For instance, investors might view larger security issues as being more likely to sustain liquid trading conditions, which would allow investors to rebalance their portfolios, as conditions evolve, at reasonably predictable prices and with transaction costs comparable to those of other securities traded in "thick" markets. In addition, as has become evident, tranched securitizations are exposed to tail risks—situations that can be expected to occur only rarely but which convey very negative returns. Numerous thin tranches may be more vulnerable to tail risks, because credit losses in the underlying loan pool may be more likely to wipe out designated cash flows for the entire tranche—so-called cliff effects. Thus, future mortgage securitizations that rely on simpler cash flows and larger tranches might reduce some of the exposure to tail risks and enable investors to gain confidence.

Third, non-agency mortgage securitization contracts contained numerous idiosyncratic features that limited the comparability of deals that may have appeared to be similarly structured. Not only might there have been subtle but significant differences in the cash flow obligations to each tranche, but there was also much variation in other important provisions of the so-called "pooling and servicing agreements," such as duties on servicers of the loans in the pool and the representations and warranties that govern the circumstances under which poorly performing loans can be put back to the originator. Greater clarity and consistency in the obligations of mortgage servicers in determining when and what types of loan modifications and principal write-downs can occur also would streamline and expedite the workout process, likely reducing foreclosures and uncertainty about the payoffs to investors. Once again, this would help to bring down the costs for market participants to do their own evaluations.

Thus, even if comprehensive data on the loans in the pools had been available, a thorough credit analysis would have required both a detailed reading of the documentation describing a particular deal's potentially unique structure and a careful analysis of how its cash flow prioritization would affect returns to holders of the particular tranches of securities as laid out in the contract. Although such an analysis is possible, it may be beyond the available resources for many investors. More homogeneous mortgage securitization contracts with fewer and less complex tranches could significantly lower the barriers to entry for credit analysts, effectively providing more competition for the credit rating agencies and promoting greater transparency and perhaps more confidence among investors about the securities' underlying risk-return attributes.

Even with all of these reforms, however, the mortgage securitization may be slow to recover due to concerns about underwriting standards in an "originate to distribute" model. Many have discussed the potential for loan originators to have less incentive to assess carefully the likelihood of repayment of a mortgage if they sell the mortgage into an MBS rather than keep the loan on their books where they would directly bear the losses (e.g., Bank of England's Financial Stability Report, 2008, Seru 2009). There continues to be a lively debate about how much loan originators may have taken advantage of their superior information about the quality of a loan to originate and sell "lemons" without those risks being properly disclosed and priced. The credibility of underwriting standards in an "originate to distribute" model certainly has been called into question and investors will require an increase in that credibility before returning to the market.

Improved data, disclosure, and modeling will be crucial, as noted above, but this is where consumer protections such as those embodied in the Home Ownership Equity Protection Act (HOEPA) rules put forward by the Federal Reserve in 2008 also can be helpful in restoring credibility and reviving the market (see Kroszner 2008a). The Dodd-Frank legislation also creates a Bureau of Consumer Financial Protection with responsibilities in this area going forward.

Mortgage borrowers, their communities, and investors as well as lenders and securitizers that wish to rebuild this market can directly benefit from sound underwriting standards and protecting borrowers from abusive practices. Practices that have hurt consumers have also undermined the confidence of investors and contributed to a virtual shutdown of the subprime market with consequences for all segments of the mortgage market as well. It is important to have active enforcement to prevent loans that strip borrowers' equity or involve unsound underwriting standards. Protecting borrowers through enforcement of sound underwriting standards also protects the integrity and proper functioning of the mortgage market by increasing investor confidence.

Sensible and effective consumer protection thus is important for revival of these markets since it can reduce uncertainty and revive the flow of credit, thereby relaxing some of the constraints that the financial crisis has put on consumer credit availability. The HOEPA rules apply to "high cost" loans, that is, subprime loans, underwritten by any type of financial institution, including banks, independent mortgage companies, or mortgage brokers. The rules prohibit a lender from granting a mortgage without taking into account the borrower's ability to repay the loan from income and assets other than the value of the house. Second, the rules require that a lender verify income and/or the value of assets that the lender relies upon to determine the borrower's repayment ability. Third, lenders must establish an escrow account for the payment of property taxes and homeowner's insurance for first-lien loans.

Such underwriting standards not only help to protect consumers from potentially abusive practices but are sensible ways to provide greater comfort to market participants who may be trying to estimate the risks associated with such lending. Such underwriting standards can help to mitigate the "lemons" problem by reducing uncertainty about "low quality" loans in the market and thereby restore credibility that mortgages sold into MBS will adhere to a minimum underwriting standard.

A mortgage securitization and structured finance market built upon significantly more detailed data disclosure, more consistent and less opaque contracts, and improved underwriting standards will help to revive the flow of credit to the mortgage market and make the market more robust to changes in market conditions.

Next I want to turn from some of the specific contract structures and market practices that made the securitization and structured finance market quite fragile to focus on institutions, particularly those that are large and interconnected through various market contracts.

Improving Resolution of Financial Institutions

Trying to define what is a systemically important institution is particularly difficult. The boundary line will change over time as market practices, products, and institutions and their relationships change. The Dodd-Frank Act empowers the Federal Reserve and the newly created Financial Services Oversight Council of regulators (of which the Fed is a member) to determine what institutions are systemically important and impose higher regulatory requirements on them.

Rather than tackle this particularly knotty question directly, I will focus on some changes that can make the failure of institutions, regardless of their size or complexity, less likely to be systemically important. The failure of any significant player in a particular market, as well as significant players in many markets, of course, can have ripple effects. The reforms I focus on here might reduce the frequency with which ripples from a failure can turn into tidal waves that can devastate a wide variety of markets and institutions. The section of the Dodd-Frank Act focused on creating a new resolution regime for systemically important institutions is motivated by these considerations.

Financial markets and institutions tend to rely quite heavily on well-developed legal and court systems. This is why uncertainties generated by bankruptcy, for example, can have a significantly larger impact on such firms than on non-financial firms. A clear example of this is the pressures that the remaining large independent investment banks were facing in the first half of September 2008. They were finding it increasingly difficult to obtain funding, either through the issuance of short-term commercial paper or in the overnight secured lending markets (tri-party repo). In addition, customers and counterparties were turning away from them. Given the inefficiencies and uncertainties of how contracts would be treated in bankruptcy, customers of the firms were concerned that insolvency of, for example, their broker could lead to their accounts being frozen, even if temporarily. When there was such high demand for liquidity, even a relatively small probability of not having the ability to trade and having some funds temporarily frozen can lead even long-standing customers to turn elsewhere.

These institutions were facing a form of a run. This was not a run by depositors as had been witnessed in the U.S. in the early 1930s, but by their funders, counterparties, and customers, with each feeding on the other. Given the uncertainty about how secure "secured" funding was, and arising at least in part from bankruptcy/legal uncertainties (particularly in terms of timing of repayment or ability to liquidate the collateral), funders were pulling back. At the same time, customers fearing the uncertainty about how their accounts/activities might be affected by bankruptcy also pulled back and began switching to competing entities with few such concerns.

In other words, the business model of these institutions was effectively imploding, and this was being driven at least in part by the uncertainties of how contracts would be treated under bankruptcy. As has been argued for many countries around the world, uncertainties about contract enforcement and property rights can reduce the willingness of investors to provide funds (e.g., La Porta, Lopez-de-Silanes, Shleifer, and Visny 1998 and de Soto 2000). In some sense, there was a parallel in the extreme circumstances of 2007 to 2009 for the United States: the uncertainties about property rights and contract enforcement in financial markets came to the fore and the consequence was a significant disruption of financial flows and freezing of markets.

An improved resolution regime for large financial institutions could help to reduce the likelihood of a ripple turning into a tidal wave and of the freezing of markets. A key goal would be to reduce uncertainty about the process, timing, and treatment of customers and claimants when an institution is insolvent or close to insolvency and to promote expedited resolution to reduce concerns about access to funds and liquidity. One approach would effectively replace the bankruptcy code, much as the FDIC's authority does now for insured depository institutions, to allow the resolution authority to become a conservator or receiver and merge the institution or transfer it to a "bridge financial company." An additional complication for non-depository institutions and holding companies is the patchwork of other resolution regimes that may apply to such institutions facing failure, including the Secured Investors Protection Act (SIPA) for brokerages, a wide variety of state laws and state resolution and insurance schemes for insurance companies, foreign statutes for internationally active institutions, and the Federal Deposit Insurance Act (FDIA) itself for depository institutions within a holding company structure. (See Paul, Weiss, Rifkind, Wharton, & Garrison, 2009.)

Providing as much clarity as possible ex ante about which types of institutions will be covered and how their financial contracts will be treated will be crucial to the success of such a resolution regime in reducing uncertainty and making markets more robust in the face of failing financial institutions. While the Dodd-Frank Act does create a new resolution regime for the systemically important institutions, the legislation itself leaves open much about how the resolution would operate in practice. If wide-ranging powers are given to government authorities to intervene and rewrite contracts without clear rules and guidance as to how various classes of creditors, counterparties, and customers would be treated, then the goals of providing clarity and reducing the likelihood of destabilizing pull-backs would not be achieved. It is thus crucial for the Treasury and the FDIC to clarify these issues if the new regime is to mitigate the problems we observed during the 2008/2009 financial crisis.

A closely related but distinct issue is the role of government assistance or support for institutions covered by this regime. Certainly the potential for moral hazard problems may be huge if there is a possibility of large amounts of taxpayer assistance with little ex ante reigning in of risks that these institutions may undertake. The ability of the resolution authority to provide assistance and the source of funding for such assistance are crucial issues. Regularizing and systematizing any such interventions once again could help to reduce uncertainty, but would have to come with safeguards to protect the taxpayer from excess exposure to private sector risk taking. The effectiveness of the new Dodd-Frank resolution regime will depend critically on how this issue is dealt with.

Various forms of "pre-packaged" bankruptcy, "living wills," and clearinghouses that can deal with failures in the derivatives markets, as described in the next section, can help to reduce uncertainty and the likelihood that concerns about bankruptcy become self-fulfilling. The Dodd-Frank Act requires a rapid resolution plan, much like a living will, for systemically important institutions (see Kashyap 2009).

A "living will" could provide a clear roadmap for how funds would flow and how various creditors, counterparties, and customers would be dealt with as an institution begins to experience difficulty but prior to bankruptcy. It would provide clear guidance to market participants and supervisors about how a large complex institution might be dismantled and how particular operations that had gotten into trouble would be wound down. To be credible, such a contract would require a significant increase in the transparency of the operation of a financial firm, e.g., less commingling of funds, greater clarity of exposures, etc. One of the challenges is differences in tax regimes across venues that can lead to greater complexity of operations and flows as financial firms try to minimize tax payments (see Tett 2009). The G-20 is encouraging its members to adopt some form of living wills.

Central-Clearing Counterparties and Clearinghouses versus Over-the-Counter Derivative Markets

A goal that is complementary to improving the resolution regime for large nonbank financial institutions is to reduce the need for and scope of such a regime, that is, to adopt policies that reduce the likelihood of being faced with the prospect of a ripple turning into a tidal wave. One potentially effective way to deal with this is by bringing derivative contracts onto platforms with centrally clearing counterparties, such as clearinghouses, to mitigate the risk that derivative markets can create a "too interconnected to fail" problem. An additional approach, as will be discussed in the next section, is to discourage contracts that have the potential to destabilize markets: for example, when the safeguards that market participants employ for their individual positions can have the unintended effect of actually exacerbating market-wide distress and amplifying losses among multiple market participants during times of market turbulence.

Clearinghouses as central counterparties can be an effective way to mitigate the potential problem of "too interconnected to fail" (see Kroszner 1999). In the nineteenth and early twentieth centuries, futures exchanges struggled with the challenges of trying to make contracts more readily tradable on the exchanges. As noted above, homogeneity of contract provisions and enforcement of a consistent commodity grading regime (e.g., winter wheat #2 instead of Farmer Jones' wheat and Farmer Smith's wheat) were crucial to enhancing the liquidity of futures markets on the exchanges. The last major step toward full fungibility of the contracts, however, was reducing and homogenizing counterparty risk. Even if all of the other features of the contract were identical, the potential for nonperformance would vary with the stability of the entity on the other side of the transaction—so called "name" risk—since the contracts were bilateral obligations between the buyer and settler.

To limit and homogenize counterparty risk, the clearinghouse came to act as a central counterparty for all of the transactions on the exchange. The clearinghouse as central counterparty generally runs a balanced book to try to avoid direct market exposure. The clearinghouse requires margin to be posted by the members and cumulates a fraction of its clearing fees in a reserve fund. In the case of a member's default, the central counterparty can draw upon the proprietary margin of the defaulting member, its own reserve fund, preestablished lines of credit, and the assessment of members for share purchase. The exchange and clearinghouse set a number of criteria for capital, liquidity, exposure limits, etc. of their members and police whether their members are in good standing. Central counterparty clearing has been quite robust to stressful market conditions, allowing them to operate successfully through the Great Depression, World War II, and the failures of major market participants.

The central counterparty structure attempts to address the problem of system-wide risk in these markets, that is, of a failure of one institution causing problems throughout the system due to cascading failures on derivatives contracts. If the central counterparty is credible in terms of the resources at its disposal to deal with failures and make good on the existing contracts, then the failure of one institution does not have consequences that ripple through the system.

Institutions become less "interconnected" in the centrally cleared derivatives contract market than in an OTC market because the central counterparty guarantees the performance on the contract. A credible central counterparty thus acts as a barrier that helps to prevent the ripples of a failure of a market participant turning into a tidal wave that can undermine other institutions.

In addition, with central clearing, there is much better information about exposures and concentration of risks. The central counterparty would quickly become aware of rapid changes in exposures of market participants and undertake actions to try to limit them. Supervisors then could much more easily monitor risk concentrations, unlike in OTC markets, and become aware of risk exposures at institutions that the supervisor may not directly regulate but that could have system-wide consequences. Central clearing thus makes it more likely that the excessive concentrations of risk can be detected and defused earlier, and thereby contribute to stability by improving the informational infrastructure of the marketplace.

Markets with a credible central counterparty also are less likely to freeze up. In March and September 2008, for example, there was concern that the failure of a major player in the credit default swaps (CDS) market could undermine confidence in all of the counterparties because the market might simply break down. Hedges "broken" when a counterparty failed then could not be replaced. In this circumstance, positions that initially appeared well-hedged could have become "naked" risk exposures—in other words, "net" positions may have become "gross" positions and institutions would not have had sufficient capital to cushion against those exposures. Without central clearing, it can be quite difficult to judge the safety and soundness of an institution. One needs to assess not only its risk exposures but the ability of its counterparties to make good on their contractual commitments. Since there is no central clearing or central record keeping, knowledge of the extent of exposure to particular counterparties is almost impossible for a funder or customer to determine. Even if that were known, one would then have to assess the safety and soundness of the counterparty, which would require knowing its exposures and the creditworthiness of its counterparties, etc. This uncertainty about counterparties' exposures and soundness led to the evaporation of confidence and to "runs" by funders, counterparties, and customers on institutions perceived as vulnerable. A credible central counterparty, however, can help to avoid such a situation because the central counterparty would make good on performance of the contracts and there would be less concern that the market would break down and that "broken" hedges could be replaced.

If central counterparty clearing has such benefits, then why has it not been adopted in all derivative markets, such as CDS? One reason is that the gain in safety may come at the expense of flexibility. A central counterparty imposes a degree of standardization upon contracts in order to make the central clearing feasible. Similarly, it may be easier to experiment and innovate OTC. Part of the reason for the rapid growth of OTC derivative markets is due to the demand for variety and customization of contracts. That said, many OTC contracts are already eligible for clearing through a central counterparty. For example, SwapClear, a central counterparty for interest rate swaps, clears about half of global single-currency swaps between dealers. The CDS that are created as indexes of individual name CDS contracts, e.g., an index of similarly rated or otherwise similarly situated firms, tend to be reasonably standardized in their structure.

A second reason may be volume and liquidity. Undertaking the costs of central clearing by market participants and managing risks for central counterparties are most feasible when there is a relatively deep and active market in the contract. For CDS, for example, the index CDS as well as individual name CDS on the largest firms account for the vast majority of trading in CDS and would be likely to have the depth to make central clearing feasible.

A third reason may be that some players in an OTC market might prefer the opacity of an OTC market compared with greater information that becomes public in an centrally cleared market about pricing, trading, etc. There were extensive discussions and debates for many years, for example, among Chicago Board of Trade members with somewhat differing interests before the Board adopted full central counterparty clearing in 1925 (see Pirrong 1997).

The Dodd-Frank Act creates a new regulatory framework that strongly encourages the movement of OTC derivatives to centrally cleared platforms and increases disclosure about exposures. It also provides a new framework for the regulation, oversight, and governance of the clearinghouses themselves. Strong incentives through differential capital charges for centrally cleared vs OTC derivatives could be given to the major players in derivatives markets to migrate existing contracts, to the extent possible, onto such platforms and to develop contracts with sufficient standardization that they can be centrally cleared. This would reduce the likelihood of institutions threatening to become "too interconnected to fail" as the supervisors and exchanges can more readily monitor the buildup of exposures and as the consequences of the failure of an institution are mitigated by the ability of the central counterparty to reduce disruption of the markets. Naturally, the extent to which the central counterparty will be successful will depend on its perceived ability to withstand the failure of key players in the market so the strength and credibility of central counterparties to manage risk in new areas such as CDS will be crucial.[3]

Potentially Destabilizing Contracts

The financial system also can be made more robust by providing improved incentives for counterparty credit risk management that operates successfully in normal times and in periods of market-wide stress. A broad class of market practices exist, for example, that can provide useful protections when an individual firm experiences trouble, but these practices may not provide useful protections—and could be potentially harmful—when the trouble is market-wide. In other words, such provisions can exacerbate so-called tail risk and destabilize institutions and markets (see Kroszner 2008e).

A representative example is the use of rating triggers in counterparty credit risk management. Some debt contracts and OTC derivative contracts link collateral requirements to a counterparty's credit rating. If a counterparty is downgraded past some threshold, it may become subject to an immediate margin call. Counterparty credit risk appears to remain contained so long as the rating trigger is breached long before the counterparty could reach insolvency—that is, the trigger is set at a relatively high rating. In such cases, this type of clause can be quite valuable in mitigating counterparty credit risk and in giving the counterparty strong incentives to try to maintain its financial health and, hence, its rating.

This type of protection against counterparty risk is most effective when changes in risk are specific to the counterparty and not correlated with increases in risks to other counterparties and in other markets. In this case, the posting of additional collateral long before a firm reaches insolvency can provide valuable protection. Such a provision may not provide protection, however, if the rating change comes too late, the firm is on the brink of insolvency, and the requirement to post the margin can push it into insolvency.

More importantly, such a provision may also fail to provide protection if the trouble at the counterparty is correlated with trouble at other institutions and in other markets, that is, due to market-wide distress. In times of widespread distress, many counterparties may have to sell assets simultaneously to post margin. This occurrence can potentially lead to a situation in the market in which assets are sold quickly and, in an illiquid market circumstance, below their fundamental values. When many counterparties are forced to liquidate similar assets, prices for those assets are pushed down. If these assets are used as collateral on other positions, then the decline in value leads to additional margin calls. This set of circumstances, in turn, forces further liquidation and price declines. A widespread use of rating triggers can accelerate this downward slide, with further losses in asset values triggering additional downgrades and requirements to post collateral and liquidate positions. This potentially destabilizing dynamic was at work during the crisis in 2008 (see Brunnermeier 2009 and Kroszner and Melick forthcoming).

Rating triggers are certainly only one example of market practices that can exacerbate the impact of a systemic event and make financial markets less stable. Credit enhancements and guarantees can also create fragility while seeming to offer protection. A highly rated guarantor, for example, could offer effective protection against the default of a small number of instruments. In the event of a market-wide increase in credit risk, however, there is an increased probability that the guarantor would be required to pay out on many positions simultaneously. As the market comes to realize that the credit enhancement may not be effective, further pressure may come upon the institutions that would be left exposed. Thus, widespread reliance on credit enhancements could induce a form of "wrong way risk" in which the seller of protection becomes most likely to default in precisely the circumstances where protection is most valued.

What might seem like "herd" behavior in some markets may be at least in part a response to the fragile interconnections affecting the stability of those markets. Such apparent herding behavior, reflecting a collective loss of confidence, may be generated by a market infrastructure that induces co-movements across markets and institutions during times of stress. In these circumstances, contractual provisions that might seem on the surface to be prudent counterparty risk management could increase financial market stress.

One way to discourage such contracts would be careful supervision of the inadequacy of such contracts to deal with—and potentially to exacerbate—tail risks. Supervisors have typically focused more on protections that covenants afford an individual firm in stressed circumstances without focusing as much on the market-wide consequences of the contracts or their lack of protection against tail events. Capital charges could be imposed to discourage such contracts. In some cases, credit enhancements can reduce capital charges, but contracts that do not protect against the type of tail risk described here should not receive preferred treatment. Codes of best practices also could be encouraged by various trade organizations to reduce reliance on or eliminate the use of contracts that have these potentially destabilizing features.

Conclusions

As noted in the introduction, I have not attempted to cover all areas of law, regulation, supervision, and market practice that could be reformed to address problems that the recent crisis has brought to prominence. Rather, I have tried to highlight a number of areas that make markets more fragile and reforms that could help to mitigate "too big" and "too interconnected to fail" problems as well as some procyclicality problems. Much of my focus has been on the institutional and legal infrastructure of the financial markets—credit rating agencies, securitization structures, bankruptcy resolution, central clearing of derivatives, and potentially destabilizing contractual structures—because they play fundamental but often overlooked or underappreciated roles in generating the confidence and stability that a financial intermediation system that relies on long chains of market-based finance needs to work most effectively.

Improving the resolution regime for large financial institutions and bringing over-the-counter derivative contracts onto platforms with central counterparties are among the highest priority reforms with the greatest scope for reducing "tail risk" and enhancing stability. The Dodd-Frank legislation does focus on these areas of reform but leaves much to be determined by the rule-making and actions of regulators and supervisors. Addressing infrastructure issues may be one of the most effective means of making markets more robust going forward.

Notes

I am grateful to Brian Barry, Benjamin Friedman, George Kaufman, Sam Peltzman, Richard Posner, Robert Pozen, Raghuram Rajan, Hal Scott, Robert Shiller, and symposium participants for helpful comments. Contact information: randy.kroszner@chicagobooth.edu.

1. On a complementary aspect of competition, Benmelech and Duglosz (2009) provide evidence that tranches of structured products rated by only one of the major agencies have been more likely to be subject to subsequent downgrade than those with multiple raters.

2. See Global Joint Initiative to Restore Confidence in the Securitization Markets, *Restoring Confidence in the Securitization Markets*, a report sponsored by the Global Joint Initiative's Steering Committee, a consortium of the Securities Industry and Financial Markets Association, the American Securitization Forum the European Securitization Forum, and the Australian Securitization Forum, December 3, 2008, www.sifma.org/capital_markets /docs/Survey-Restoring-confidence-securitization-markets.pdf.

3. Pirrong (2008/2009) raises questions about whether the resources and risk management of central counterparties, which have proved so resilient for so many exchange-traded derivatives, will be able to handle new OTC contracts such as CDS.

References

Adrian, Tobias, and Hyun Song Shin. 2009. Money, Liquidity, and Monetary Policy. *American Economic Review* 99 (2):600–605.

Bank of England. 2008. Financial Stability Report. London.

Benmelech, Efriam, and Jennifer Dugloz. Forthcoming. The Credit Rating Crisis. Forthcoming in the NBER Macroeconomics Annual, Cambridge, M.A.

Blankfein, Lloyd. 2009. "Do Not Destroy the Essential Catalyst of Risk." *Financial Times (North American Edition)*. February 8.

Brunnermeier, Markus. 2009. Deciphering the Liquidity and Credit Crunch 2007-08. *Journal of Economic Perspectives* 23 (1):77–100. http://www.princeton .edu/~markus/research/papers/liquidity_credit_crunch.pdf.

Calomiris, Charles. 2009. "Financial Reforms We Can All Agree On." *Wall Street Journal*. April 23, p. A17.

de Soto, Hernando. 2000. *The Mystery of Capital: Why Capitalism Triumphs in the West and Fails Everywhere Else*. New York: Basic Books.

Diamond, Douglas, and Raghuram Rajan. 2009. The Credit Crisis: Conjectures about Causes and Remedies. *American Economic Review* 99 (2) (May): 606–610. http://faculty.chicagobooth.edu/brian.barry/igm/thecreditcrisisdoug .pdf.

Financial Stability Board (FSB). 2008. "Report of the Financial Stability Forum on Addressing Procyclicality in the Financial System," Bank for International Settlements, April.

Financial Stability Board (FSB). 2009. "Report of the Financial Stability Forum on Enhancing Market and Institutional Resilience," Bank for International Settlements, April.

Friedman, Jeffrey, ed. 2009. "Causes of the Crisis" issue of *Critical Review* 21 (2–3). Oxford, U.K.: Routledge Press.

Gorton, Gary. 2009. "Slapped in the Face by the Invisible Hand: Banking and the Panic of 2007." Yale School of Management. http://papers.ssrn.com /sol3/papers.cfm?abstract_id=1401882.

Kashyap, Anil. 2009. "A Sound Funeral Plan Can Prolong a Bank's Life." *Financial Times (North American Edition)*. June 29.

Kroszner, Randall 1999. Can the Financial Markets Privately Regulate Risk? The Development of Derivatives Clearing Houses and Recent Over-the-Counter Innovations. *Journal of Money, Credit, and Banking* (August): 569–618.

Kroszner, Randall. 2008a. "Protecting Homeowners and Sustaining Home Ownership." Presented at the American Securitization Forum. Las Vegas, Nevada. February. http://federalreserve.gov/newsevents/speech/kroszner 20080204a.htm.

Kroszner, Randall. 2008b. "Liquidity-Risk Management in the Business of Banking." March 3. http://www.federalreserve.gov/newsevents/speech /kroszner20080303a.htm.

Kroszner, Randall. 2008c. "Strategic Risk Management in an Interconnected World." October 20. http://www.federalreserve.gov/newsevents/speech /kroszner20081020a.htm.

Kroszner, Randall. 2008d. "Improving the Infrastructure for Non-Agency Mortgage Backed Securities." December 4. http://federalreserve.gov /newsevents/speech/kroszner20081204a.htm.

Kroszner, Randall. 2008e. "Assessing the Potential for Instability in Financial Markets." December 8. http://federalreserve.gov/newsevents/speech /kroszner20081208a.htm.

Kroszner, Randall. 2010. "Interconnectedness, Fragility, and the Crisis." Statement to the Financial Crisis Inquiry Commission. Washington, D.C. February. http://www.fcic.gov/hearings/pdfs/2010-0226-Kroszner.pdf.

Kroszner, Randall, and William Melick. Forthcoming. The Response of the Federal Reserve to the Recent Banking and Financial Crisis. In *An Ocean Apart? Comparing Transatlantic Response to the Financial Crisis*, ed. Adam Posen, et al. Washington, D.C.: Petersen Institute for International Economics.

La Porta, Raphael, Florencio Lopez-de-Silanes, Andrei Shleifer, and Robert Visny. 1998. Law and Finance. *Journal of Political Economy* 106 (6): 1113–1155.

Paul, Weiss, Rifkind, Wharton, & Garrison LLP. 2009. "Treasury Proposes New Resolution Authority for Systemically Significant Financial Companies." New York. April 10.

Pirrong, Craig. 1997. The Inefficiency of U.S. Commodity Manipulation Law: Diagnosis and a Proposed Cure. In *Research in Law and Economics*, eds. Richard O. Zerbe Jr. and William Kovcic. Volume 18. New York: JAI Press.

Pirrong, Craig. 2008/2009. The Clearinghouse Cure? *Regulation Magazine* 31 (4) (Winter): 44–51.

Posner, Richard A. 2009. *A Failure of Capitalism: The Crisis of '08 and the Descent into Depression*. Cambridge, M.A.: Harvard University Press.

Rajan, Raghuram. 2009. "Too Systemic to Fail: Consequences, Causes, and Potential Remedies." Testimony before the Senate Banking Committee. University of Chicago Booth School of Business. May 9. http://banking.senate .gov/public/index.cfm?FuseAction=Files.View&FileStore_id=40ba6d40-c960 -4abe-82d0-d41cbd0b028f.

Securities and Exchange Commission (SEC). 2005. "Proposed Rule: Definition of Nationally Recognized Statistical Rating Organization." April 19.

Seru, Amit. 2009. *Did Securitization Lead to Lax Screening? Evidence from Subprime Loans*. Chicago: University of Chicago, Booth School of Business, working paper.

Shin, Hyun Song. 2008 "Reflections on Modern Bank Runs: A Case Study of Northern Rock." Princeton University. August. http://www.princeton.edu /~hsshin/www/nr.pdf.

Shin, Hyun Song. 2009. "Financial Intermediation and the Post-Crisis Financial System." Presented at the Eighth Annual BIS Conference.

Tett, Gillian. 2009. "Why the Idea of a Living Will Is Likely to Die a Quiet Death." *Financial Times (North American Edition)*. August 14.

3 Comments

BENJAMIN M. FRIEDMAN

The papers by Robert Shiller and Randall Kroszner present two interesting contrasts. Shiller takes a more fundamental approach, envisioning an Internet-style open-source, or bottom-up, structure of how the financial markets ought to work, while Kroszner takes a much more pragmatic (as he labels it) objectives-based, market-oriented approach. And while Kroszner's paper reflects an underlying confidence in the ability of market competition to perform its presumed economic role of generating outcomes that we would not only identify as equilibria but characterize as economically optimal—in many cases, he argues, our recent problems were due to an *absence* of competition—Shiller, in line with a number of his recent works (his *Irrational Exuberance*, for example, and also his more recent *Animal Spirits*, written with George Akerlof), emphasizes instead the tendency of competitive market settings to produce what everyone would recognize, at least after the fact, as neither an equilibrium nor an optimal outcome.

Despite these contrasts in fundamental approach, however, what most strikes me about the two papers is the commonality of the positive recommendations that Shiller and Kroszner offer. Their shared view of what we need to do now, coming as it does from their quite different orientations, is, I think, highly significant. In particular, it suggests that we have arrived at a juncture at which the way forward has many elements that arise in common, despite differences in mode of argumentation and even underlying philosophy, so that that these prior doctrinal, and often political, disagreements need not be an impediment to making progress in the policy arena.

Reading across the two papers, we find two basic rationales for financial regulation. Shiller argues mostly at the micro level, calling for what he terms a "psychological self-control mechanism" (p. 8), not in the sense that one individual, a Robinson Crusoe alone on his island, might also need a psychological self-control mechanism, but rather emphasizing what happens when individuals—buyers, sellers, and others—interact in a social (that is to say, a market) context. Kroszner emphasizes, in addition, the moral hazard problem introduced by the inevitability of government assistance and bailouts: inevitability because he too, like Shiller, rejects the notion that we could eliminate problems such as those we have recently experienced simply by making clear in advance that the government would never step in to assist a troubled institution and then relying on the self-policing forces of the private sector to do the job. In Kroszner's view, bailouts and assistance are inevitable; and therefore so too is the moral hazard problem that they create, and so also is the need for regulation to address it.

In addition to Shiller's focus on psychological tendencies and Kroszner's on moral hazard, a third element I think is worth making explicit is that a large part of the behavior of financial institutions that has been at the root of our recent difficult experience is a consequence of the basic principle of limited liability. When we talk about capital requirements, for example, what underlies the entire line of inquiry is that under limited liability neither the shareowners in an enterprise nor the debt holders are called upon to put up additional monies in the event of a failure. This institutional arrangement holds, of course, in many circumstances ranging well beyond the financial sector. But what magnifies its importance for financial institutions is the parallel fact of high leverage, so that the liability that is limited turns out to be, indeed, very limited: in the case of American investment banks in recent years, capital equal to only some three percent of the activity on the firms' balance sheet, not to mention all of the off-balance-sheet obligations, and in the commercial banking sector normally only about eight percent. Limited liability per se creates a form of moral hazard problem, and would do so even if there were no possibility at all of the bailouts and other forms of assistance that Kroszner emphasizes.

Shiller writes that "the free market is one of the most important inventions in human history. It is indeed an invention, and the invention takes the form of regulation and standards enforced by some form of government. Markets and government are thus inseparable" (p. 14). In light of the political polarization surrounding much of today's discussion of what to do about our collapsed financial system, it is perhaps worth pointing out that this line of thought is very much one of which Adam Smith—yes, that Adam Smith—would have approved. It sometimes seems as if most of the people who today go around citing Adam Smith have heard of *The Wealth of Nations* but never read it, and have never even heard of Smith's other works. (Smith favored, for example, strict limits on interest rates—in other words, usury laws—as well as restrictions on the instruments banks could issue to fund themselves.) The thought that Shiller has expressed here, the fundamental

interconnection between markets and government, was a
major theme of Smith's *Lectures on Jurisprudence*, in which he
argued that one of the most important consequences of what
he and his contemporaries called commerce, namely the combination of specialized production and voluntary exchange,
was precisely that this form of economic activity called into
existence, *because it required them*, certain forms of government
institutions and government interventions: most obviously,
arrangements like contract enforcement, a monetary system,
and standardized weights and measures, but many others be-
sides. Although Shiller does not refer to Smith in making his
argument, it is valuable in today's politicized environment
to recognize that the supposed tension between the functioning of the market and the role of government in its enabling
regulatory capacity is not one that Adam Smith would have
recognized.

Shiller goes on to make the corollary point that it was largely
the combination of deregulation and a reluctance to enforce
what regulation we still had that led us to the financial collapse, as well as the enormous economic costs this collapse
has brought. But we should also be prepared to ask why the
failure of regulation occurred. I think there are several reasons
to which one can point. One, of course, is political: the long
arc from Roosevelt's acceptance of the role of government to
the Reagan/Thatcher view that government is never a solution, only the problem itself. Second, there was an ideological
view—these days personified by Alan Greenspan, with his
early dedication to the writings of Ayn Rand and especially
his strongly antiregulatory stance while leading the Federal
Reserve System—that private market–driven economic activity is not only self-regulating but, when necessary, self-
correcting. Shiller introduces a third, equally important reason
for this failure: that it also had intellectual origins.

Shiller's argument is that ideas are fundamentally important and that, albeit with a lag, the ideas of researchers, including economic researchers, help drive thinking in the practical sphere and from there end up driving thinking about public policy as well. Ironically, as he points out, in this case academic research—specifically, thinking about the efficient markets hypothesis—had begun to change some years ago. But importantly, the process of influence that he emphasizes is subject to a lag; although academic thinking on this subject had begun to turn years earlier , as he notes, ideas in the world of public discussion had turned more recently, and ideas in the policy sphere had yet to do so.

What should our policymakers do now? Because what impresses me most about these two papers is the commonality of their positive recommendations, despite the differences in their respective underlying orientation, I will highlight here some of the ideas that they put forward that seem to me to lead to further questions. First, both Shiller and Kroszner are strongly in favor of something that we could call a systemic risk regulator. But what is the role of that systemic risk regulator? In principle, the Dodd-Frank legislation has now created just such a body, in the new Financial Services Oversight Council. But what should the Council do? In Kroszner's interpretation, the main point is to take steps that will arrest contagion once a crisis begins. In Shiller's interpretation, the role of the systemic regulator is, in addition, to anticipate, in a forward-looking way, the development of bubbles. These are very different roles. Thinking of both together, simply as endorsing the idea of a systemic regulator such as the one Dodd-Frank created, makes the commonality seem more than it is.

A second key issue revolves around accounting rules and capital requirements. A question that repeatedly figures in much of today's discussion is whether to eliminate hedge funds. A hedge fund, by definition, is an investment fund that stands outside of the prevailing regulatory apparatus. If it were within the regulation that requires holding capital against risk positions, for example, then it would no longer be a hedge fund (at least not by today's standard definition). Should we—indeed, in light of how markets operate internationally, could we—make hedge funds illegal?

Third, it is important to underscore the treatment, in both of these papers, of the hard issue of data availability. In the case of mortgage-backed securities (MBS), for example, there is no obligation for the trustees of these assets to make available the granular data on the underlying mortgage loans, and in practice most do not do so. Even if someone wanted to do the research needed to evaluate the likelihood of repayment of the underlying loans, in many cases it would be impossible to get the necessary data. Moreover, there is no evidence that Moody's or Standard & Poor's, or any of the smaller rating agencies that evaluated these securities, ever raised an objection to this unavailability of data. Moody's, for example, has been straightforward in explaining that in rating these securities it did not have the information even to know where the houses, the mortgages on which were packaged into the securities they were rating, were located.

Finally, I want to turn to an issue that repeatedly comes up in these papers: the role that the Federal Reserve System has played in directly acquiring privately issued obligations and in guaranteeing the values of privately issued obligations that it does not acquire. We all hope, of course, that the assets the Federal Reserve has acquired will retain their values, and that the guarantees the Federal Reserve has given that remain outstanding will never be called. But what happens if some of those assets do lose value, and some of the guarantees are called? Then, in effect, the central bank will turn out to have been conducting fiscal policy. And depending on the size of the losses, it was at least possible from the commitments made that it would turn out to have been doing so on a grand scale.

At one level, everybody understands this; much of the relevant public discussion today takes for granted that the Federal Reserve has been called upon to play this role precisely because neither the Bush Administration nor the Obama Administration was willing to ask Congress for the funds, beyond what was already authorized in the Troubled Asset Relief Program (TARP), to finance these asset purchases and guarantees. But what this means is that not only is the central bank carrying out a form of fiscal policy, but the reason for its doing so is an awareness that if the normal Constitutional requirements that fiscal policy go through the Congressional appropriations procedures were invoked, Congress would not agree.

What then happens if markets take a turn such that the Federal Reserve takes losses on its holdings of privately issued obligations and if the guarantees it has issued are called? There would surely be a reaction against the notion that the central bank, in this extra-Constitutional fashion, has been carrying out a fiscal policy that everybody knows Congress would not have approved. The likely political reaction, I fear, would be steps to limit the future ability of the central bank to act. To be sure, it would be desirable if that political reaction were sufficiently refined that it merely precluded the Federal Reserve from again embarking on what amounts to a "shadow fiscal policy," while continuing to respect and maintain the central bank's independence with regard to monetary policy—which is, after all, its primary responsibility. Political reactions, however, are rarely this refined. A potential cost of the Federal Reserve's engaging in this shadow fiscal policy, therefore, is that it potentially places in jeopardy the central bank's independence with respect to monetary policy as well. From the perspective of most students of monetary policy, that would be a very serious cost indeed.

GEORGE G. KAUFMAN

Both of these two interesting papers focus on ways of improving the performance of financial markets in the United States to avoid repeating the ongoing financial crisis in the future and on strengthening consumer protection. But they take different approaches. Shiller emphasizes the "need to invent new rules of the game" (p. 1) to save the capitalistic system through "democratizing" and "humanizing" finance (p. 4). Kroszner emphasizes steps to improve the efficiency of markets in five specific areas through a better understanding of what went wrong and how to repair it. Kroszner produces a more cold-blooded, analytical (Chicago School) approach compared to Shiller's warmer and fuzzier approach. Shiller wants to incorporate animal spirits into the new framework, while Kroszner wants to harness these spirits. My comments will focus primarily on the Shiller paper as it was received earlier, is more controversial, and provides a natural lead into the Kroszner paper.

Shiller develops an analogy for financial markets in the form of a sports game with players, rules, and referees who enforce the rules. He argues that the current problem arose because the rules are broken and the referees cannot do their job well. I will propose an alternative hypothesis, namely that the problem arose not so much because the rules were either broken or inadequate but because the referees did not enforce the rules well. The regulators had their own agenda, which at times conflicted with the objectives of the rules in place. Thus, they often were poor agents for healthy financial institutions and taxpayers. The basic underlying problem is a serious principal–agent problem.

In recent papers, I have identified a long list of culprits and villains among both players and referees in Shiller's game who share responsibility for the turmoil.[1] They are housed in all sectors—private and public. There were both market and regulator (but not necessarily regulation) failures. As Pogo noted, "we have met the enemy and they are us." The 2007 financial meltdown was a perfect storm. If any of the identified culprits had not been present, the financial disturbance would have been considerably milder. In my previous papers, I grouped the culprits in alphabetical order as:[2]

- Central bankers (monetary policy)
- Commercial bankers
- Financial engineers
- Government (congress and the administration)
- Investors / ultimate lenders
- Mortgage borrowers
- Mortgage brokers and salesmen
- Prudential bank regulators

In this brief comment, I will focus only on the U.S. referees, who had the responsibility for enforcing the U.S. rules. Downturns and crises expose sins that exist but are mostly covered up in good or boom times when asset prices increase and few investors in these projects request withdrawals. As Warren Buffet noted, it is "only when the tide goes out that you can learn who's been swimming naked." Sins accumulate during booms until the last one is one too many and breaks the camel's back. In 2007, the last straw was the end of the housing price bubble.

Shiller and the Sins of the Referees

Perhaps most importantly, the prudential regulator referees allowed banks to maintain insufficient regulatory capital (permitted excessive leverage), particularly in a bubble environment. Some even argued that there was too much capital in the banking system, not too little. With rare exception, they opposed both higher regulatory capital requirements and the simple leverage ratio, which was binding for many large U.S. banks, as a measure of capital adequacy, in favor of more complex risk-weighted capital ratios. For the largest banks, the regulators were willing to adopt solely the advanced internal ratings proposal of Basel II, which would have lowered their regulatory capital requirements, on average. Moreover, work on the complex Basel II regulatory capital requirements diverted the attention of many of the brightest minds in the agencies, as well as in academe, banking, and consulting firms, from working on a number of the important issues discussed below.[3]

The agencies were insufficiently concerned with financial stability. The U.S. was almost the only industrial country to neither publish a financial stability report nor participate in the IMF–World Bank financial sector assessment program.[4] Although no U.S. regulatory agency was specifically charged with preparing such a report, neither was there a provision preventing them from doing so. The logical agency would have been the Federal Reserve, which has umbrella regulatory and supervisory authority over bank holding companies. If an agency had done this, it would have both extended its vertical analysis to large financial institutions beyond banks and generated much interesting and informative horizontal data across institutions that might have been helpful in deciphering what was happening in the financial sector as a whole and, at minimum, issuing warnings about any increasing fragility and implications for the macroeconomy.

The agencies were unprepared to resolve insolvent large "systemic" financial institutions and deal with potential contagious adverse spillover. This contributed to the depth of the crisis. Large bank resolutions are complex, both because the institution may operate in more than one country and each jurisdiction has its own resolution regime and because the resolution regimes in the U.S. differ for banks and nonbanks, which include parent bank holding companies and many of their nonbank subsidiaries. Insolvent commercial banks may be resolved pretty much seamlessly with little or no interruption in the provision of major services. Insolvent nonbank financial institutions generally cannot be.

At times, bank regulators may be unwilling to impose losses on some or all uninsured depositors or other creditors of an insolvent bank. The agencies have resolved many large insolvent banks in different ways in terms of both timing and loss allocation. As a result, banks and bank holding companies are uncertain about how their insolvency would be resolved and are unlikely to operate in the most efficient manner. Some agencies claim, with little evidence, that they did conduct resolution "war games" but were unwilling to share this information with the public for fear of starting a bank run. But secret resolution regimes do not carry the day! They do not reveal the rules of the game and thus do not affect the behavior of institutions in a desirable and predictable way.

The regulators have failed to aggressively enforce the prompt corrective action (PCA) provisions of the Federal Deposit Insurance Corporation Improvement Act (FDICIA) of

1991 and, on occasion, have permitted and even participated in known violations. The Inspector General of the Department of the Treasury recently identified six occasions in which parent holding companies of thrift institutions regulated by the Office of Thrift Supervision (OTS) were permitted by the agency to backdate the timing of a down-streamed capital injection, so as to avoid or delay the imposition of sanctions on the institutions, including possible closure.[5] The agency practiced forbearance. Two of these institutions were subsequently closed with an estimated loss to the FDIC of some $15 billion.

Specifically in recognition of the tendency for bank regulators to forbear, many of the sanctions under PCA were made mandatory when designated capital ratio triggers were hit. FDICIA also requires the regulators to legally close an insured institution and place it in receivership, when its equity drops below 2 percent of its assets, at least cost to the FDIC. The underlying theory is that if an institution is legally closed before its capital turns negative, losses are limited to its shareholders. Depositors and other creditors are protected and deposit insurance would effectively be redundant. But losses to the FDIC in recent resolutions of insolvent institutions have averaged over 20 percent of total assets, suggesting significant delayed intervention and forbearance.

One of the reasons that the current crisis is so severe is that the number of securities indirectly affected by the problems in the subprime mortgage market was both vastly underestimated and the ownership of the securities largely unreported. This was particularly true for complex structured mortgage securities, such as collateralized debt obligations (CDOs), and for credit default swaps (CDSs). Banks effectively sold the cash flows from their mortgage loans to off-balance sheet entities, such as structured investment vehicles (SIVs), that used the pooled flows to create CDOs. These were in turn sold in the capital market. But the banks retained an unreported implicit liability. If subsequent credit problems with these securities threatened the reputation of the bank, the bank brought the securities back on its own balance sheet. Moreover, the issuing bank frequently kept only the highest rated AAA senior tranches of the CDOs it sold, rather than the lowest rated junior tranches, which require more intensive hands-on credit monitoring that may have caught problems sooner.

The total volume of CDSs on a particular bond frequently greatly exceeded the underlying number of outstanding bonds. This occurs because, just as in off-track betting, where betters need not be at the race track, economic agents can trade CDSs on bonds that they do not own. The agencies had the authority to collect limited data on these securities from bank holding companies and, with the cooperation of other, nonbank regulators, from insurance companies and possibly other major nonbank financial institutions. But they did not do so.

The Home Ownership and Equity Protection Act (1994) gave the bank regulators authority to regulate much of the mortgage industry, including questionable and abusive origination practices. But the regulators did not propose comprehensive corrective actions until 2008 and did not propose lower leverage through higher down payments.[6] It should be noted that even if they had, such proposed restrictions would likely have encountered significant opposition from both the industry and Congress and may not have been promulgated.

The agencies diagnosed the crisis initially in the summer of 2007 as a liquidity problem rather than a solvency problem and primarily initiated policies to increase liquidity in the perceived impacted markets. These policies focused on channeling additional funds into these markets and guaranteeing transactions to increase both the volume of trade and security prices. It was only later that the agencies admitted that the lack of trading also reflected uncertainly about the financial solvency of counterparties and initiated actions to increase bank capital levels. In part, this delay reflected the reluctance of regulators to recognize bank failures on their watch. They are charged to protect bank safety and failures represent a black mark on their record. This delay in recognizing the problem correctly and designing appropriate policies likely deepened the crisis and delayed recovery.

The regulators also opposed requiring mandatory subordinate debt issuance by (at least) large banks. The market interest rates on these credibly uninsured securities would reflect the market's evaluation of the risk of bank failure and could be used by regulators to supplement their own information or feed directly into the PCA structure to trigger sanctions.[7] In addition, changes in the market interest rates on the sub-debt are likely to modify bank management behavior in directions that would reduce risk.

Lastly, regulators exempted debt and preferred stock issued by housing GSEs from diversification and risk restrictions. National and many state-chartered banks are prohibited from lending to any one borrower aggregate amounts in excess of 15 percent of their capital and from investing in stock in general. But exceptions were made to both restrictions for GSEs. When Fannie Mae and Freddie Mac both failed in 2008, a number of primarily smaller banks recorded large losses.

This is not to argue that, had the regulators undertaken most or all of the actions enumerated above, the crisis would have been prevented. Probably not, but its magnitude might have been smaller. Moreover, the imposition costs of these actions would have been relatively small and would easily pass a cost–benefit calculation. In 2009, the U.S. regulators began making 180 degree reversals in some of these sins. They have announced the need for higher regulatory capital requirements, particularly in good times, for placing greater emphasis on the leverage ratio, and for participation in the IMF–World Bank financial sector assessment program. These policy changes did not affect the rules of the game, but primarily the referee's enforcement of the existing rules or their intent.

Kroszner

In his paper, Kroszner analyzes and offers recommendations for improvement in efficiency in five areas:

· Credit markets

· Revitalizing securitization markets

· Nonbank financial institutions resolution regimes

· Central clearing party (CCP) or clearing house (CH) for many over-the-counter (OTC) derivative securities and

· Counterparty contracts for swap and other credit derivative contracts.

All five of these areas are important and Kroszner's analysis helps to call additional much-needed attention to them. None of his recommendations appear unduly controversial or likely to attract much opposition, although, as noted earlier, extending bank insolvency resolution provisions to large nonbank financial institutions and bank holding companies may be more complex than many proponents perceive.

The real question is why were these issues not addressed earlier, particularly by the regulators? The New York Federal Reserve Bank did call attention to the poor state of back office for OTC CDSs and encouraged the transition to CHs, but moved so slowly that, while paperwork was greatly improved by 2008, clearing was not. In addition, despite the widely accepted criticisms of the rating agencies and their ratings, the

Fed relied on them in its own Term Asset-Backed Securities Lending Facility (TALF) program.

Probably the most interesting and challenging of Kroszner's proposals are those for reviving the securitization market and for modifying counterparty derivative contracts. The former needs to overcome both a bad rap and the usual innovation risk, which exists with the introduction of almost any new product, be it the steam engine, airplanes, or corporate junk bonds. The last were the subprime mortgage bonds of the 1980s and are now, 20 years later, accepted as an integral and lasting part of the corporate bond market. Securitization is an important innovation that promises large, lasting welfare gains if done right. To do so requires learning the lessons from the errors of recent years. The need to modify counterparty derivative contracts, particularly the implications of closeout on systemic risk, was pretty well missed by the regulators, who argued for such provisions until recently. These contracts require fixing.[8]

Conclusion

Why do we study the past? An optimist would say to avoid repeating the same errors. As the late Spanish-American philosopher George Santayana (1863–1952) noted, "those who cannot remember the past are condemned to repeat it." But I find this observation not to be very interesting as most policymakers I have met remember at least some of the past. Unfortunately, this leads me to conclude more generally that "those who can remember the past are condemned to agonize first and then to repeat it." And that is what appears to have happened in the events leading up to the current crisis. Responding to the crisis, we must be careful, as Kroszner notes, not to "throw out the baby with the bathwater" that elevated us to the high level of economic welfare we currently enjoy even after the crisis. We must also be careful, paraphrasing the words of a U.S. combatant in the Vietnam War, not to "destroy the economy in order to save it."

Notes

1. Kaufman (2009).

2. I omit academics, although they are on the whole also guilty for not seeing either the current crisis coming or its depth when it did come.

3. Kaufman (2006 and 2007).

4. Oosterloo et al. (2007), p.340. The other industrial country to not issue a report was Italy.

5. Thornson (2008) and Hopkins (2009).

6. Bair (2009).

7. Shadow Financial Regulatory Committee (2000).

8. Bliss and Kaufman (2006).

References

Bair, Sheila C. 2009. "Statement before the Committee on Banking, Housing and Urban Affairs." U.S. Senate. Washington, D.C. March 19.

Bliss, Robert R., and George G. Kaufman. 2006. Derivatives and Systemic Risk: Netting, Collateral, and Closeout. *Journal of Financial Stability* 2 (1) (April):55–70.

Hopkins, Cheyenne. 2009. "Treasury IG Faults OTS for Allowing Backdating." *American Banker*. May 22.

Kaufman, George G. 2006/2007. "Basel Has Been a Costly Distraction on the Road to Minimizing the Societal Cost of Bank Failures." Power Point presentation at FDIC conference, Washington, D.C., September 13, 2006 and Working Paper, Loyola University Chicago, July 10, 2007.

Kaufman, George G. 2009.The Financial Turmoil of 2007-0X: Causes, Culprits and Consequences. In *Financial Crisis Management and Bank Resolution,* eds. J. Raymond LaBrosse, Dalvinder Singh, and Rodrigo Olivares-Caminal. London: Informa Publishers.

Oosterloo, Sander, Jacob De Haan, and Richard Jong-A-Pin. 2007. Financial Stability Reviews: A First Empirical Analysis. *Journal of Financial Stability* 2 (4)(March):337–355.

Shadow Financial Regulatory Committee. 2000. "Reforming Bank Capital Regulation." Statement 160. Washington, D.C.: American Enterprise Institute. March 2.

Thornson, Eric M. 2008. "Letter to Senator Grassley." Washington, D.C: U.S. Treasury Department. December 22.

ROBERT C. POZEN

I am pleased to comment on these two papers by such distinguished economists: a broad, almost philosophical paper by Professor Shiller and a paper by Professor Kroszner with specific reform proposals. I will begin by addressing two key issues in Professor Shiller's paper—democratizing investing and regulatory structures. Then I will respond to Professor Kroszner's specific proposals in three main areas—credit rating agencies, mortgage securitization, and credit default swaps (CDS).

I   Professor Shiller's Paper

I will take up a few of the most interesting points made by Professor Shiller on democratizing investment opportunities and redesigning regulatory structures.

A   Democratizing Investing Opportunities

Professor Shiller is a passionate advocate for allowing average people to participate more actively and intelligently in the investment process. He would like to see average people participate in relatively complex investment vehicles like hedge funds and the new partnerships to purchase toxic assets from banks. However, he recognizes that average people may need assistance from experts in certain cases, and therefore wants to promote the use of financial advisers.

1   Investor Education

A key predicate to many of Shiller's ideas is better education for investors. While I strongly support investor education, I may be more realistic about its limits. The mutual fund industry, for example, has spent years developing investor friendly materials such as a summary chart of yearly fund expenses and returns. After a decade, the Securities and Exchange Commission (SEC) has finally agreed to a summary prospectus—an outline of the critical points for an investor deciding whether to buy a mutual fund. In addition, fund investors have easy access to a vast array of comparative analyses of mutual funds through online and paper services such as Lipper or Morningstar.

However, many investors often do not read the information provided to them, even if presented in summary or tabular forms. Some investors rely primarily on funds rated with four or five stars by Morningstar. The behavior of other investors is heavily influenced by inertia, as Richard Thaler and others have shown (2008). For instance, the percentage of employees participating in 401k plans at work is much higher if employees are asked to "opt out" of these plans, rather than "opt in." In other words, many employees do not get around to filling out an application form for a 401k plan despite their stated desire to save more for retirement.

Recognizing these limits to investor choice, many 401k plans now employ an opt-out procedure, combined with a balanced fund or set of lifestyle funds as a default investment option. A default is needed since many investors do not make any investment choice. Further, this type of self-adjusting default option is needed because most investors do not rebalance their 401k funds on an annual basis, despite receiving educational materials urging them to do so.

2 Financial Advisers

Professor Shiller correctly points out that tax laws currently disfavor deductions for financial advice. Expenses for financial advice may be deducted only if they exceed 2 percent of a filer's adjusted gross income. For instance, a family with adjusted gross income of $80,000 may not deduct the expenses of hiring a financial adviser except to the extent that those expenses exceed $1,600 per year. This 2 percent minimum is too high for most investors.

The SEC's rules on financial advisers to individual investors are more complex. Many private offerings of securities are done without an SEC registration in reliance on SEC Rule 506. This rule allows an issuer to offer securities of any amount to thirty-five or fewer investors subject to certain conditions. Most importantly, the thirty-five must generally be "accredited investors"—with a net worth of at least $1 million or at least $200,000 per year in income. However, SEC Rule 506 (b)(2)(ii) allows non-accredited investors to participate if the investor "alone or with his purchaser representative(s) has such knowledge and experience in financial and business matters that he is capable of evaluating the merits and risks of the prospective investment..."

By contrast, the SEC exemptions for hedge funds do not contemplate a role for financial advisers. Hedge funds could not generally live with the leverage limits and other restrictions required of collective investing pools registered under the Investment Company Act of 1940. Instead, most hedge funds come within a registration exemption in Section 3(c)(7) of the Investment Company Act of 1940, which applies to a fund making a nonpublic offering to fewer than 500 "qualified purchasers." This term is defined in Section 2(a)(51) of the Investment Company Act to mean that an investor must have $5 million in investable assets (excluding the investor's home). For example, an individual with $1 million in portfolio assets would probably be excluded from a hedge fund even if he or she had a sophisticated financial adviser. Thus, the SEC should amend its rules to allow an accredited investor plus a financial adviser to be deemed a qualified purchaser under Section 3(c)(7) of the Investment Company Act.

B Regulatory Structure
Professor Shiller is quite critical of the current structure of U.S. financial regulation, especially the duplication of functions among agencies. He is also a general skeptic about the benefits from deregulation.

1 Regulatory Mergers
In support of his case for merging agencies, Shiller cites the three regulatory objectives delineated by former Treasury Secretary Henry Paulson: systemic risk, prudential regulation, and business conduct. Shiller is right in pointing out the difficulties of one agency conducting both consumer protection and prudential regulation—the latter seems to take priority. (Perhaps for this reason, the Dodd-Frank law created the new Bureau of Consumer Financial Protection administratively within the Federal Reserve System but not subject to Federal Reserve oversight.) However, these three objectives are insufficient to guide the design of an optimal regulatory system. Most importantly, every agency engages in risk control—usually in addition to prudential regulation and consumer protection—so these objectives can be just the first steps in designing regulatory structures.

A more useful criterion may be the relative expertise of an agency in organizing prudential regulation or consumer protection, together with a risk control function, in a specific financial service. It would make sense under this criterion, as Shiller suggests, to bring together in one federal agency all mortgage-related functions that are scattered throughout the federal bureaucracy—e.g., in the Federal Reserve, the Federal Trade Commission and, most recently, a joint state-federal registration system for mortgage lenders.

By contrast, it would not make sense under this criterion to combine the regulation of mortgage origination, credit cards, and mutual funds in one consumer products commission. (The new Bureau of Consumer Financial Protection has purview over some aspects of mortgage origination and credit cards, but not mutual funds.) Yes, they are all three financial products sold mainly to financial advisers, but the products involve very different expertise and processes. Mortgage origination is a shared federal-state function in which roughly half of mortgage lenders are not banks. Mutual funds are SEC-registered products sold by national brokers and banks across the country. It would be highly inefficient to duplicate securities expertise in another federal agency other than the SEC. Similarly, credit cards are now products issued mainly by national banks across the country. Again, it would make little sense to develop banking expertise on credit cards in yet another agency.

2 Deregulation Issues

Shiller expresses criticisms about various deregulatory measures, including the repeal of the Glass Steagall Act (now replaced, albeit in a limited way, by the "Volcker Rule" in the Dodd-Frank legislation). In his critique, Shiller joins others who argue that the repeal of the Glass Steagall Act was a major cause of the financial crisis. However, this argument is weak for several reasons.

First, before the repeal of the Glass Steagall Act, banks had for years been allowed to engage in many securities activities, such as buying corporate bonds and mortgage-backed bonds. Bank holding companies were also allowed to underwrite stocks and bonds through a Section 20 subsidiary as long as these activities were limited to 25 percent of the subsidiary's total revenues. The repeal of Glass Steagall in 1999 meant primarily that banks themselves could engage in securities underwriting.

Second, highly rated portfolio holdings of mortgage-backed bonds were the main cause of losses to banks during this financial crisis. If the securities underwriting of these banks had been a major problem, we would have expected them to be left holding the lowly rated securities that could not be sold to investors in underwritings. Instead, banks generally incurred large losses on the triple-A tranches of mortgage-based bonds held in their investment portfolios.

Finally, Glass Steagall never applied to the securities activities of U.S. banks outside the U.S. It would be even more impractical now to reinstate the Glass Steagall limits on securities activities of U.S. banks. With the increase in globalized securities markets, it would be even easier for U.S. banks to use offshore operations to conduct their securities underwriting.

II Professor Kroszner's Paper

I will take up three of the most innovative proposals put forward by Professor Kroszner in his paper.

A Credit Rating Agencies

After recounting the many deficiencies of credit rating agencies, Kroszner argues that more competition is the key to reforming these agencies. It is true that credit ratings for structured products were dominated by an oligopoly of Moodys, S&P, and Fitch. However, the fundamental defect of the credit rating agency model was that issuers can shop around to get a better rating if the initial agency selected were not receptive to the rating. If this is the fundamental defect, tripling the number of SEC recognized agencies would only aggravate the problem of forum shopping.

Kroszner noted one of the problems with switching to a model where investors pay for ratings. He points out, for example, that certain investors might have an incentive to inflate the rating to investment grade to satisfy legal requirements— e.g., on state pension plans. More fundamentally, the largest institutional investors would refuse to pay for a credit rating because they do their own research on bonds, which they believe is superior to the analytic work of the credit raters.

So what remedy might work to cure forum shopping? In my view, the SEC should put together a pool of independent financial experts who would perform only two functions for each major bond offering—select a credit rating agency and negotiate the cost. The expert would be chosen by the SEC, but the expert's standard fee would be paid by the bond issuer. Although not a perfect solution, the intervention by the expert would eliminate the two worst abuses of the credit rating process—biased selection and excessive fees to obtain a higher rating than warranted.

B Transparent Securitization

Although many have called for more transparency in the process of securitizing mortgages, Kroszner has a few concrete and new suggestions. One good suggestion is to offer fewer and larger tranches in private-label mortgage-backed securities (MBS). As Kroszner points out, such tranches should be more liquid and less vulnerable to tail risks. A second good suggestion is more standardization in the servicing agreements, especially in cases of loan modifications. This suggestion would, for example, clarify the role of the servicer in loan modifications under the Obama Administration's recent programs. A third good suggestion is more standardization of mortgage contracts for the securitization process. In fact, there might have to be several standards forms, such as one for adjustable-rate mortgages and another for fixed-rate mortgages. A further suggestion might be to simplify the structure of MBS deals. With hard work, analysts can understand the issuance of several tranches of MBS based on one discrete pool of mortgages—especially if the SEC insisted on better disclosure of individual loans in the pool. However, it is quite difficult to analyze multi-layer collateralized debt obligations (CDOs)— that is, when the CDO invests in tranches of MBS from many different pools, rather than in the mortgage pools themselves. In such multi-layer CDOs, even a small error in estimating default rates on mortgages in the underlying pools can lead to very large errors in estimating the default rate at the top CDO layer.

C CDS Clearinghouse and Exchanges

Kroszner suggests that the trading of CDSs be done on exchanges and clearinghouses. These are both sensible responses to the systemic risks created by the current system of trading CDSs in the privately negotiated over-the-counter (OTC) market. However, it is important to separate and prioritize these initiatives—in my view, a central clearinghouse should be a substantially higher priority than exchange trading for CDS.

As Kroszner points out, a clearinghouse limits the systemic risks of failure by either party to a CDS contract. The clearinghouse requires the relevant party to post margin, which would be adjusted daily by the clearinghouse in light of price movements. If a party defaults, the clearinghouse would close out the contract and cover any shortfall by that party's margin deposit and, if insufficient, by a reserve fund created by contributions from all members.

By contrast, trading CDSs on exchanges would increase transparency and reduce spreads. While these are both laudable goals, they are less important than reducing systemic risks from the failure of a party to a CDS contract. Moreover, there is a political consensus on the need for a CDS clearinghouse, but a heated debate on whether standardized CDSs should be traded only on an exchange. The OTC dealers in CDS contracts strongly oppose exchange trading of CDSs because it conflicts with their economic interests. It would be unfortunate if the much needed establishment of a CDS clearinghouse were delayed due to a political debate about exchange trading of CDSs. A central clearinghouse can integrate exchange and OTC trades, as shown by the clearing mechanism for U.S. stocks.

III Conclusions

The papers of Professors Shiller and Kroszner put forward several creative and sensible ideas for financial reform. I hope their ideas will be taken seriously in Washington, D.C. in the debate over further financial reforms after Dodd-Frank.

Reference

Thaler, Richard, and Cass Sunstein. 2008. *Nudge: Improving Decisions about Health, Wealth and Happiness*. New Haven: Yale University Press.

HAL S. SCOTT

Systemic Risk Reduction

Both these papers agree that a central problem for regulation going forward is to reduce systemic risk. In my view this is by far the most important objective. The threat of systemic risk (whether real or just imagined) results in the need for government bailouts at taxpayer expense and an increase in moral hazard, since both equity and debt holders are protected against losses. Of course, the government could just not intervene, but this could put the entire global economy at risk, an even worse outcome. As Shiller points out, however, populist political reaction—how can you bail out the banks?—may limit what the government (Treasury or even the Fed) can do. I want to address what I believe are the three most important features for dealing with systemic risk discussed in these papers: capital requirements (or limits on leverage), the use of clearinghouses and exchanges, and resolution of insolvent institutions.

Capital Requirements

Capital requirements have been the chief ex-ante measure to reduce systemic risk. Capital requirements are designed to decrease the likelihood of bank failure. Without bank failures (or more properly financial institution failures), the problem of systemic risk largely disappears. Capital requirements have been highly regulated for a long time, and since 1988 internationally through the Basel Committee on Bank Supervision. The United States implemented Basel I and is in the process of implementing Basel II for banks and their holding companies—the Securities and Exchange Commission (SEC) had already implemented Basel II for securities firms' holding companies before the onslaught of the credit crisis.

It is fair to say that these capital requirements have proven completely inadequate. The SEC's Basel II rules permitted the top five major investment banks to achieve an average leverage of over thirty-to-one. The lack of capital was a major reason for the failure of Lehman and the government-assisted takeover of Bear Stearns. Lack of adequate capital also played a major role in the necessity for Merrill to sell out to Bank of America. Yes, liquidity was also a problem, but so was inadequate capital. Indeed, the most intensive and detailed area of regulation, capital, has not worked. More regulation does not necessarily translate into less systemic risk.

One of the ironies of the capital regulation story is that the leverage of banks turned out to be much less than the investment banks—the top five commercial banks were levered at an average of thirteen-to-one, due to a leverage ratio requirement. Whereas Basel imposed an 8 percent capital requirement against risk-weighted assets, the leverage requirement of 5 percent was imposed against total assets without risk weighting. The leverage ratio turned out to be a more binding restraint on banks than the more "sophisticated" Basel approach.

There have been many suggestions for changes in capital regulation to fix the problem, e.g., dynamic provisioning along the lines in Spain, or contingent capital plans to address the cyclicality of existing requirements, but no one has addressed the most fundamental issue—how much capital we should require banks or other financial institutions to have. Basel I backed into the 8 percent requirement in 1988 out of a desire not to increase bank capital as a result of the implementation of its new regime, and Basel II basically took the same approach. But can regulation really determine what the right amount of capital is?

Another difficult problem is how to define capital. Basel defines Tier I capital, which must be at least 50 percent of total capital, differently than tangible common equity, the capital measure investors seem to be focused on today. The main difference between the two is that Basel ignores bank equity losses resulting from marking to market available-for-sale assets, on the theory that mark-to-market losses do not fairly portray bank capital—this is highly questionable but it raises the key issue of whether there should be differences between regulatory and accounting measures of capital and, if so, what they should be.

Given the regulatory failures and the difficult challenges of ever designing an effective regulatory regime for capital, I think we should explore more use of market forces in addressing the capital problem for publicly traded financial institutions. If the market had better information about the riskiness of financial institutions and could bear some risk for their failure through holding an "unbailable" credit like subordinated debt, market forces could be harnessed to impose more discipline.

Clearinghouses and Exchanges

Kroszner's paper rightly focuses on the role that clearinghouses can play in reducing systemic risk. If a financial institution fails, it may result in losses for counterparties on in-the-money derivatives contracts. If these counterparties do not have adequate collateral, they may also fail, and their counterparties may fail as well, and so on. A clearinghouse can reduce this risk by expanding netting and collectivizing losses through becoming the counterparty to each contract. Thus, the impact of the failure of one institution is borne by all the members of the clearinghouse, not just by individual counterparties. Of course, the result is risk to the clearinghouse, which then needs to take measures to reduce its own risk, and Kroszner spells out these measures in his paper. The first line of defense is margining requirements for out-of-the-money participants.

I believe clearinghouses can reduce but not eliminate systemic risk. There is still a risk of clearinghouse failures despite their own risk prevention measures, and there is little doubt that the government would bail out a clearinghouse if it is already willing to bailout systemically important institutions. So these clearinghouses need to be carefully regulated—as they are today—but even then the risk of clearinghouse failure remains.

Another problem with the completeness of the clearinghouse solution is that it can only clear standardized contracts. Although over-the-counter (OTC) derivatives contracts are becoming more standardized, they are still marketed as customized solutions for clients. For example, on credit derivatives, parties can choose how they define "Credit Events," the occurrence of which triggers a settlement obligation. Nonstandardized contracts cannot be netted or priced for the purpose of setting margin requirements. Should we mandate standard derivative contracts to solve this problem?

Other issues with clearinghouses are: how many should there be and what derivatives contracts should they clear? Duffie and Zhu[1] have pointed out that one may achieve more risk reduction through bilateral counterparty netting and collateral for all derivative contracts than one would get from a centralized clearing of just credit derivatives, yet the clearinghouses under way like IntercontinentalExchange (ICE) are focused only on credit derivatives. And how many should there be? One clearinghouse is more efficient but its failure poses more systemic risk.

Perhaps the mostly highly contested issue is whether there is a need for derivatives to be exchange traded over and above the need for clearinghouses. Dealers are generally opposed to exchange trading for business reasons—it would narrow their spreads—but there is a legitimate issue of policy as to whether exchange trading is desirable or feasible. The argument for exchange trading is that it would improve the ability to price derivatives—which is important not only to traders but to the clearinghouse as well in setting margin requirements. However, currently, pricing information, with respect to quotes, is available to the clearinghouse from vendors like Markit on both an end-of-day and intraday basis. On the other hand, there is no current intraday collection of pricing data based on transactions; indeed only 60 percent of trades are reported to the Depository Trust & Clearing Corporation (DTCC) Warehouse by the end of the day. An exchange would provide constant data on the prices of transactions.

Exchanges may also improve liquidity—again this is not only important to traders but also to a clearinghouse seeking to close out a position of a defaulting member. It would do so by taking offsetting trades to lock in overall losses. It would seem likely that an exchange would add liquidity to that presently achievable in the OTC market. But also bear in mind that the class of derivatives that would be exchange traded is a subset of those that would be cleared through a clearinghouse, due to inadequate volume to attract trading interest. To conclude, while clearinghouses and perhaps exchanges can play an important role in reducing systemic risk, substantial systemic risk from counterparty default is likely to remain.

Resolution Procedures

The amount of systemic risk associated with insolvent financial institutions can be affected by how we deal with them. At present we may be reluctant to allow insolvent institutions to fail because of how they would be dealt with once they failed. Thus, the fear of how the Bankruptcy Code handles derivatives contracts—it basically results in counterparties liquidating collateral (which can trigger failures as the value of all collateral is driven down)—appears to be a major reason why authorities have sought to avoid bankruptcy for systemically important institutions, including bank holding companies. This was also a major consideration in the creation of the AIG receivership structure.

It might well be that the Troubled Asset Relief Program (TARP) and some liquidity infusions into bank holding companies that would otherwise be insolvent are designed to avoid forcing these institutions into bankruptcy. But this in turn necessitates taxpayer losses or increased risk to the Fed. We need a resolution procedure for all financial institutions that would allow flexible ways to deal with derivatives contracts and at the same time permit restructuring of debt. The Dodd-Frank legislation directs the new Financial Services Oversight Council to advise the Federal Reserve on improving resolution procedures, but it remains to be seen what concrete steps either of these entities will take.

Conclusions

Systemic risk reduction is the most important area for regulation, but regulation alone cannot solve the problem. It is not clear that more regulation will achieve systemic risk reduction, as evidenced by our experience with capital requirements. Limiting interconnectedness through the clearinghouse and possibly exchanges is clearly necessary, but this is not only an issue of regulation (although clearinghouses need to be regulated). It is also a matter of having a prudential command (in this case from the New York Fed) in the market to find ways to reduce interconnectedness. Finally, we need better resolution procedures. This is also not just a matter of regulation (a prescription of rules). It also involves the devising of legal structures like bankruptcy laws.

So regulation plays a role, but so should the market, prudential direction, and legal structure. Even then, we must be prepared to live with some level of potential systemic risk.

Note

1. Darrell Duffie and Haoxiang Zhu, "Does a Central Clearing Counterparty Reduce Counterpart Risk?" Rock Center for Corporate Governance of Stanford University Working Paper No. 46, February 27, 2009.

4 Responses

ROBERT J. SHILLER

I am very pleased to see the range of ideas raised here by Randall Kroszner and the four discussants, who are some of our greatest thinkers on financial reform.

Two of the discussants—Benjamin Friedman and George Kaufman—note a fundamental difference between my piece here and that of Kroszner. In Friedman's words, while Kroszner takes a "pragmatic . . . objectives-based, market-oriented approach," I take a "fundamental approach" aimed at describing how things "ought to work" (p. 85). Kaufman says Kroszner takes "a more cold-blooded, analytical (Chicago School) approach" while I take a "warmer and fuzzier approach" (p. 92). I believe the essence of the difference between my proposals and those of Kroszner may relate to our different views about how human beings make decisions, and consequently what kinds of regulations are needed to affect decision making. In Kroszner's view, humans are largely rational and analytic, while in my "warmer and fuzzier approach," I believe we must take into account the possibility that, at least at times, men and women make decisions based on irrational, emotionally based thinking.

As George Akerlof and I assert in our 2009 book *Animal Spirits*, issues of fairness and over- and under-confidence at times drive human economic behavior. Yes, it is true that consideration of these kinds of factors makes models "fuzzier" and that models that ignore these factors are cleaner and simpler, but we have learned the hard way that simplicity does not necessarily lead to good policy. To me, the issue lies herein, for the financial crisis was in fact very much caused by these fuzzier aspects of human behavior, aspects that are very hard to manage and control. For this reason, behavioral economics has to be an important part of economic theory, and especially so in helping us to understand the recent financial crisis.

In fact, it is to me striking that the real source of the crisis lies in some aspects of human behavior that are not adequately captured in the canonical model. It lies, for example, in the fact that so sophisticated a financial professional as Jamie Dimon, president of JPMorgan Chase & Co, admitted in his January 2010 testimony before the Financial Crisis Inquiry Commission that "Somehow we just missed, you know, that home prices don't go up forever."[1] In retrospect, this seems like a pretty basic error from an otherwise highly sophisticated person, but Dimon was far from alone in this viewpoint. The source of the crisis lies, too, in what Carmen Reinhart and Kenneth Rogoff used as the title for their new book, something they call the "this time is different syndrome."[2] The syndrome they refer to arises if people don't learn adequately from past catastrophes, if they are able to dismiss the relevance of past events because they are distant in time, they involve other people, and if people tend to be overconfident in the leaders they have today.

The "fuzzier" aspects of human thinking are also important in understanding what is going on today in the aftermath of the crisis. There is a powerful sense of anger and of unfairness that is developing in some quarters of this country as foreclosures and layoffs continue. The anger is exemplified by the "tea party" movement and talk of a "second American revolution," and might derail any broader efforts to revive the economy if it is not dealt with constructively. Proposals to fix the economy cannot be conducted at such an abstract level that people's emotional response to damage done by the crisis is ignored.

In my paper, I stressed that in reacting against such issues, we need to democratize and humanize finance. That is, we must bring the power of financial risk management to the people so they can use it as effectively as possible, given human limitations, and so that they are not taken advantage of. From this viewpoint, when we look at the long list of proposals that are out there (Kroszner points out that the April 2009 Financial Stability Board report alone had over sixty proposals to fix the financial system) we may find most of them offer possible improvements, but there is considerable disagreement about the ranking of their importance. Of Kroszner's proposals, the most salient to me is that for consumer protection. He calls for "active enforcement to prevent loans that strip borrowers' equity or involve unsound underwriting standards," a protection that would have the effect of "increasing investor confidence "(pp. 66–67). That is right on target. It is aimed at preventing the kind of errors that have left millions of homeowners in foreclosure now. It is getting right at the sense of anger that envelopes much of our country today. Some of these ideas are in effect included in the Dodd-Frank Act. I have argued that we need even more of such protection, including the improved financial advice that I proposed.

Others of Kroszner's proposals seem very sensible, too, if not quite so high on my ranking. It is eminently sensible to devise better resolution procedures. Indeed, secured funding became insecure in this crisis because of bankruptcy uncertainties leading to a sort of run on a variety of financial institutions that used short-term financing. Kroszner is right to consider that we might extend Federal Deposit Insurance Corporation (FDIC) resolution practices to more institutions, and that we make permanent the Primary Dealers Credit Facility. This was a temporary measure set up only for "unusual and exigent" circumstances. Dodd-Frank has followed up on the first of these proposals, but the Primary Dealers Credit Facility has been shut down.

He is also right that we might consider government incentives to encourage wider use of clearinghouses, and that we should consider the systemic effects of capital triggers depending on ratings declines. These are proposals that still need to be worked on after Dodd-Frank.

We do have a significant disagreement about the proposal that Kroszner ranks first but that I would rank last. Kroszner proposes to extend competition in the rating agency industry by encouraging "fewer and larger tranches in private-label MBS" (p. 64); he asserts that this step would make them easier to analyze. I don't believe that doing this would effect any meaningful simplification or do much to correct the rating agency errors that led to this crisis. In my view, the rating agency errors were more of the Jamie Dimon variety than based on a misunderstanding of complex tranches.

Bob Pozen and Hal Scott have made some important proposals here, also. Scott expands on the clearinghouses and better resolution procedures that were discussed by Kroszner and adds a discussion of capital requirements. Pozen proposes the clever idea that the Securities and Exchange Commission (SEC) should arrange for a pool of independent experts who would choose to which agency a security would be sent for rating, thereby stopping the rating shopping. We are making a lot of progress here in terms of proposals. I hope that some of these can be implemented. Still, I am left wondering why the core problems in human behavior that led to the massive bubbles in the stock market, housing market, energy market, and commodities markets and that are leading in the aftermath of these bubbles to the strong sense of popular anger afloat today aren't talked about more with regard to fixing the financial system.

Notes

1. First Public Hearing of the Financial Crisis Inquiry Commission, January 13, 2010, p. 60, http://www.fcic.gov/hearings/pdfs/2010-0113-Transcript .pdf.

2. Carmen A. Reinhart and Kenneth Rogoff, *This Time is Different: Eight Centuries of Financial Folly*, Princeton: Princeton University Press, 2010.

RANDALL S. KROSZNER

Bob Shiller has written a wide-ranging and thoughtful paper that touches on a number of important issues. While my paper is more focused on specific reform proposals, I am broadly comfortable with his big pictures themes of "humanizing" and "democratizing" credit. When I was at the Federal Reserve Board, I chaired two committees of the Board, one on Supervision and Regulation and the other on Consumer and Community Affairs. While there, I emphasized that it was imperative to do thorough consumer testing in order to make disclosures as understandable as possible to actual consumers (see Kroszner 2007).

Pages of fine-print legalese may fulfill a statutory requirement but may cause confusion and be useless to real people. Through testing, we learned a lot about what information consumers comprehend and how the format and presentation of information matters. In credit card statements, for example, putting all of the fees in one section and summing those fees made it much easier for people to understand the costs they were incurring and compare those with other card issuers. The proposals and rules we promulgated under the Truth in Lending Act (sometimes known as Reg Z) were motivated by these types of findings and were very much consistent with the themes of humanizing and democratizing credit. Although consumer testing is a common practice in the private sector, it was novel for a federal regulator to rely upon extensive interviews and testing to improve the effectiveness of disclosures.

I also share Bob's concerns about regulatory fragmentation and the importance of the so-called "shadow" banking system. As I emphasized in my contribution to this Symposium and elsewhere (Kroszner 2010; Kroszner and Melick 2010), the financial system has evolved into an interconnected web of markets and institutions. Regulatory reform must acknowledge that reality and the fragilities of such a system. Fragmented regulation and supervision only add to those vulnerabilities, as illustrated by the subprime crisis. The federal bank supervisors, for example, in 1999 and then more extensively in 2001 (long before I arrived at the Federal Reserve) put out regulatory guidance on subprime mortgage lending. An unintended consequence of this was to provide an incentive for subprime lending to be undertaken by institutions that were not federally supervised. Mortgage brokers and other organizations grew rapidly, much more rapidly than the resources provided to their state-level supervisors.

Going forward, it will be valuable to improve information sharing among supervisors and focus supervision not only on individual institutions but on markets and the inter-linkages among institutions and markets. In any healthy and innovative financial system, new organizations, instruments, and markets will develop. Monitoring and assessing the risks, not just in banks but in the system more broadly, is important. This is precisely why I emphasize in my paper reforms focused on making markets more robust.

On the role of past regulatory changes in creating the crisis, however, I have a different perspective than Bob. In particular, he seems to attribute part of the crisis to deregulation relaxing some of the 1933 Glass-Steagall Act separations between commercial banking and investment banking. (In particular, the 1999 Gramm-Leach-Bliley Act removed the prohibition on a bank or financial holding company from owning subsidiaries engaged in securities underwriting and brokerage.) I don't see how the experience of the last few years would provide support for this point of view.[1]

The fragilities did not arise primarily from the mixing of commercial and investment banking at individual institutions. Recall that Bear Stearns, Merrill Lynch, and Lehman Brothers were not commercial bank holding companies and so their troubles had nothing to do with allowing commercial and investment banking to occur in the same holding company. The exposures that led to the downfall of IndyMac, Washington Mutual, and Wachovia, for example, were primarily related to risky choices and concentrations within the traditional commercial banking sphere of mortgage origination and lending, again not related to investment banking activities of underwriting or dealing in securities. In addition, reintroducing a Glass-Steagall separation in the U.S. would likely result in greater fragmentation of the financial system, with the likely consequence of increasing rather than decreasing the interconnectedness of banking institutions and funding sources of other financial institutions and markets. Pushing risk-taking activities just outside of the commercial banking system could have the unintended consequence of making the entire system more, rather than less, fragile.

I will now turn to some very brief remarks responding to the four discussants, whom I thank for their insightful comments and analyses.

Friedman: I am perhaps a bit less fatalistic about bailouts and moral hazard than Ben's thoughtful comment might suggest. I believe that we have to face the problem squarely and realize how difficult it is to eliminate, but I do think that reforms can significantly reduce the likelihood of bailouts and mitigate moral hazard. My approach is not simply to have ex-post responses to reduce costs of bailouts, but ex-ante changes in the legal, contractual, and information infrastructure that can significantly reduce the fragilities of an interconnected system. A better resolution regime and migrating over-the-counter (OTC) derivatives to a centrally cleared platform, for example, are ways to try to reduce the likelihood of "funding runs" and to reduce spillover effects of the failure of individual institutions. With reforms such as these, policymakers can become more comfortable with allowing an institution to fail and, thus, markets will take that into account, thereby mitigating moral hazard.

Ben also makes a very intriguing remark about the moral hazard problem that arises in any system with limited liability. Interestingly, before the creation of the Federal Deposit Insurance Corporation (FDIC), most states in the U.S. had some form of extended liability for directors and/or shareholders of banks. "Double liability" was common; that is, shareholders might be called upon to pay the par value of their shares in order to pay off the depositors of an insolvent bank. In some countries today, such as Brazil, top officers and directors have some form of extended liability.

Kaufman: I'm very glad George thinks that my proposals are sensible and noncontroversial. If only lawmakers around the world agreed! So far, the G-20 process has been slow in moving such reforms forward. George rightly asks why some of these reforms were not undertaken earlier, but the current regulatory reform debate illustrates how challenging these can be. Improving and streamlining the resolution regime requires not only changes to the bankruptcy codes domestically but international accords and protocols to ensure a clear and orderly wind-down of an international institution. The focus in the G-20 seems to be much more on capital requirements which, while important, are only one arrow in the quiver.

Pozen: As my comments above make clear, Bob and I certainly agree that it is very difficult to pin blame for the recent crisis on Glass-Steagall deregulation. We also agree that improved transparency is crucial to the revival of the securitization market. I like his proposal for further simplification of mortgage-backed securities and believe it should be taken quite seriously. I'm a bit less sanguine about having the Securities and Exchange Commission (SEC) assign "independent financial experts" to rate securities for a standard fee (p. 108). Although that certainly eliminates forum shopping, I'm not sure how the SEC could ensure the quality and fitness of those experts over time and whether a "standard" fee would ensure sufficient effort is undertaken by the assigned expert in complex and difficult cases. Finally, I am very sympathetic to his view that the first priority should be to move

OTC derivatives onto centrally cleared platforms rather than try to have full exchange trading. The key benefits for making markets more robust follow from having the clearinghouse as counterparty.

Scott: Hal focuses on the importance of capital to insure that institutions have "skin in the game," but he very rightly emphasizes the difficulty of knowing what the "right" level of capital is. If the requirement is set too low, it may not have any impact. If it is set too high, it can lead to precisely the sort of avoidance behavior we witnessed with the creation of off-balance-sheet vehicles that were not truly off balance sheet. In addition, if such subterfuges can be eliminated, then it simply leads to the activities being undertaken by other institutions that are still connected to the banks, potentially making the system more fragile.

Hal shares my view of the value of central clearing in OTC derivative markets but correctly warns that clearinghouses increase the robustness of the system only to the extent that they are perceived as completely sound. I concur. I also share his view that the objective of changes in the resolution regime must be to reduce uncertainty and improve clarity, and many of the proposals do not.

Note

1. The historical evidence also does not support an argument in favor of the Glass-Steagall separation (see, for instance, Kroszner and Rajan (1994) and Kroszner (1996)).

References

Kroszner, Randall. 1996. The Evolution of Universal Banking and Its Regulation in Twentieth Century America. In *Universal Banking: Financial System*

Design Reconsidered, eds. Anthony Saunders and Ingo Walter. Chicago: Irwin, 70–99.

Kroszner, Randall S. 2007. "Creating More Effective Consumer Disclosures." May 23. http://federalreserve.gov/newsevents/speech/kroszner20070523a .htm.

Kroszner, Randall S., and William Melick. Forthcoming. The Response of the Federal Reserve to the Recent Banking and Financial Crisis. In *An Ocean Apart? Comparing Transatlantic Responses to the Financial Crisis*, ed. Adam Posen, et al. Washington, D.C.: Peterson Institute for International Economics.

Kroszner, Randall, and Raghuram Rajan. 1994. Is the Glass-Steagall Act Justified? A Study of the U.S. Experience with Universal Banking before 1933. *American Economic Review* (September):810–832.

5 Rejoinder

ROBERT J. SHILLER

Randall Kroszner says that I seem to "to attribute part of the crisis to deregulation relaxing some of the 1933 Glass-Steagall Act separations between commercial banking and investment banking" (p. 125). He infers that I would support a reinstatement of the Glass-Steagall Act. Robert Pozen, in his comments, makes a similar inference. However, I do not favor reinstating the Glass-Steagall Act. This impression is especially important now that Dodd-Frank has implemented aspects of the "Volcker Rule."[1] Paul Volcker, former Chairman of the Federal Reserve Board, had proposed that banks should be prohibited from investing in or sponsoring a hedge fund or private equity fund or from engaging in proprietary trading. Volcker's proposal is often described as an updated version of the Glass-Steagall Act.

I do think that the Glass-Steagall Act of 1933 made some sense at the time, though it was not optimal even then. It is often forgotten that this was the act that created the Federal Deposit Insurance Corporation (FDIC). If the government was now in the business of insuring bank deposits, it would also need to take some steps to prevent excessive risk taking by the insured. Insurance creates a moral hazard that can result in losses to insurers. The insurer has the need to limit such moral hazard in this case, just as fire insurers inspect insured facilities against fire hazards.

But, we are living in a different world now than that of 1933, and we have a much better understanding of the measurement and control of risk. Kroszner is right that the very simple measure of separating investment banking from commercial banking would not address their problems well, and would not have prevented this financial crisis. Fortunately, Dodd-Frank did not take such a strong measure. Deregulation in a broader sense was part of the cause of the crisis in that regulatory gaps appeared over the years that needed attention. It was never a question of "more" versus "less" regulation. It is all a question of the quality of regulation and the sensitivity of regulation to basic principles of financial theory. The lesson should not be that we should move to an earlier era of tighter regulation, but instead that we should refine our rules to allow financial innovation to proceed constructively.

I think that Kroszner and I agree that regulation should be opening the door to new and better financial structures, structures that use our best technology to serve the people, not to impose clumsy barriers and restrictions.

Note

1. See Paul Volcker, "How to Reform our Financial System," *New York Times*, January 30, 2010. Robert Pozen has criticized proposals to reinstate Glass-Steagall in his important new book *Too Big to Save: How to Fix the U.S. Financial System*, New York, Wiley, 2010. Hal Scott did not mention it in his comments here, but he has made a substantive criticism of Glass-Steagall and the proposed Volcker Rule. See Hal S. Scott, "Prepared Written Testimony before the Committee on Banking, Housing, and Urban Affairs," United States Senate, February 4, 2010.

Contributors

Benjamin M. Friedman   William Joseph Maier Professor of
Political Economy, Harvard University

George G. Kaufman   John F. Smith, Jr. Professor of Finance
and Economics, School of Business Administration, Loyola
University Chicago

Randall S. Kroszner   Norman R. Bobins Professor of Economics, Booth School of Business, University of Chicago

Robert C. Pozen   Chairman, MFS Investment Management

Hal S. Scott   Nomura Professor of International Financial
Systems, Harvard Law School

Robert J. Shiller   Arthur M. Okun Professor of Economics,
Yale University

Index